ASIA BOND MONITOR

SEPTEMBER 2025

ASIAN DEVELOPMENT BANK

6 ADB Avenue, Mandaluyong City, 1550 Metro Manila, Philippines
Tel +63 2 8632 4444; Fax +63 2 8636 2444
www.adb.org

ISBN 978-92-9277-436-3 (print); 978-92-9277-437-0 (PDF); 978-92-9277-438-7 (e-book)
ISSN 2219-1518 (print), 2219-1526 (PDF)
Publication Stock No. SGP250355-2
DOI: http://dx.doi.org/10.22617/SGP250355-2

Note:
ADB recognizes "China" as the People's Republic of China; "Hong Kong" as Hong Kong, China; "Korea" as the Republic of Korea; "Vietnam" as Viet Nam; and "Hanoi" as Ha Noi.

Cover design by Erickson Mercado.

Contents

Emerging East Asian Local Currency Bond Markets: A Regional Update

Executive Summary vi

Developments in Regional Financial Conditions 1

Bond Market Developments in the Second Quarter of 2025 13

Recent Developments in ASEAN+3 Sustainable Bond Markets 24

Policy and Regulatory Developments 31

How Sovereign Sustainable Bond Issuance Shakes Up the Corporate Sustainable Bond Market: Evidence from Developing Asian Markets 34

Market Summaries 38

- People's Republic of China 38
- Hong Kong, China 41
- Indonesia 43
- Republic of Korea 45
- Malaysia 47
- Philippines 49
- Singapore 51
- Thailand 53
- Viet Nam 55

Emerging East Asian Local Currency Bond Markets: A Regional Update

Executive Summary

Recent Developments in Financial Conditions in Emerging East Asia

Between 2 June and 29 August, financial conditions in emerging East Asia improved, supported by continued monetary easing by regional central banks and progress in trade deals with the United States (US) in several regional economies.[1] Increased expectations of a policy rate cut in September by the US Federal Reserve, easing tensions surrounding the wider conflict in the Middle East, and an extension of the trade truce between the People's Republic of China (PRC) and the US also helped sustain positive investor sentiment in the region.

Financial market indicators largely strengthened in emerging East Asian markets during the review period. Yields declined on both 2-year and 10-year government bonds in most regional markets. Between 2 June and 29 August, risk premiums, as captured by credit default swap spreads, narrowed across the region by 9.4 basis points (bps) from 59.7 bps to 50.3 bps (simple average) and by 8.3 bps from 52.9 bps to 44.6 bps (gross-domestic-product-weighted average). The region's equity markets gained 10.8% (simple average) and 13.0% (market-weighted average) during the review period, supported by USD35.0 billion of net equity portfolio investments. Regional currencies remained stable during the review period, with a marginal appreciation of 0.6% versus the US dollar (gross-domestic-product-weighted average).

The risk outlook for regional financial markets remains balanced. While regional central banks signaled their scope for further monetary easing, investor sentiment could be negatively impacted by downside risks fueled by uncertainty over (i) US tariff policies such as sectoral tariffs and trade negotiations between the PRC and the US, (ii) the pace and direction of US monetary policy beyond the September Federal Open Market Committee meeting amid continued above-target inflation and signs of weakness in economic performance, and (iii) geopolitical tensions that could threaten supply chains. Extreme weather events such as the typhoons that occurred in the PRC and the Philippines during the review period highlight additional risks to financial conditions. A box in this issue of the *Asia Bond Monitor* provides evidence of how disasters can push up bond yields.

Recent Developments in Local Currency Bond Markets in Emerging East Asia

At the end of June, local currency (LCY) bonds outstanding in emerging East Asian markets reached USD28.6 trillion. Supported by improved financial conditions, the region's LCY bond market expanded by 3.0% quarter-on-quarter (q-o-q) in the second quarter (Q2) of 2025, compared to 2.7% q-o-q in the preceding quarter. The corporate bond stock (USD9.4 trillion at the end of June) increased by 2.1% q-o-q in Q2 2025, up from 0.9% q-o-q growth in the first quarter (Q1), on increased issuance amid continued monetary policy easing by most of the region's central banks. The region's government bond stock (USD18.5 trillion at the end of June) increased by 3.7% q-o-q in both Q1 and Q2 2025, supported by sustained government issuance to meet fiscal needs in most regional markets. Aggregate LCY bonds outstanding in member states of the Association of Southeast Asian Nations (ASEAN) increased by 1.0% q-o-q to USD2.6 trillion, comprising 9.1% of the regional total. At the end of June, 54.9% of outstanding Treasury bonds in the region carried tenors of more than 5 years, resulting in a size-weighted average tenor of 8.8 years. Banks, insurance, and pension funds remained the largest investor groups in the region's Treasury bond market, collectively holding 63.9% of the total Treasury bond stock at the end of June.

As financial conditions improved, LCY bond issuance increased by 14.8% q-o-q to USD3.1 trillion in Q2 2025, reversing the contraction of 0.6% q-o-q in Q1 2025. The rebound in issuance was supported by increased bond sales in both the government and corporate bond segments. Government bond issuance (USD1.4 trillion)

[1] Emerging East Asia is defined to include member states of the Association of Southeast Asian Nations plus the People's Republic of China; Hong Kong, China; and the Republic of Korea.

increased by 18.3% q-o-q as governments continued to front-load their funding needs and support economic stimulus measures. Corporate bond sales (USD1.0 trillion) surged by 25.2% q-o-q as companies took advantage of lower borrowing costs following rate cuts by many regional central banks. LCY bond issuance in ASEAN markets tallied USD653.8 billion, accounting for 21.1% of the regional total.

Recent Developments in ASEAN+3 Sustainable Bond Markets

Supported by benign financial conditions, robust issuance led to growth in the ASEAN+3 sustainable bond market accelerating to 3.3% q-o-q in Q2 2025 from 0.5% q-o-q in Q1 2025.[2] At the end of June, sustainable bonds outstanding in ASEAN+3 markets reached USD955.3 billion, accounting for 18.3% of the total global stock. The expansion of ASEAN+3's sustainable bond market in Q2 2025 outpaced that of the European Union 20 (EU-20) (3.1% q-o-q) and the global market (2.6% q-o-q). The share of sustainable bonds in the general bond market, however, was higher in the EU-20 (8.5%) than in ASEAN+3 (2.4%) at the end of June. Meanwhile, the sustainable bond stock of ASEAN markets totaled USD100.4 billion, representing 10.5% of the ASEAN+3 sustainable bond total and exceeding ASEAN's share of 5.9% in the ASEAN+3 general bond market.

Sustainable bond issuance in ASEAN+3 picked up to USD79.6 billion in Q2 2025 from USD49.5 billion in Q1 2025. Supported by lower borrowing costs, ASEAN+3 sustainable bond issuance grew 60.6% q-o-q in Q2 2025, rebounding from a 21.2% q-o-q contraction in Q1 2025 and surpassing issuance growth in the EU-20 (23.1% q-o-q) and the global market (6.5% q-o-q). ASEAN accounted for 6.1% of ASEAN+3's total issuance during the quarter, exceeding its corresponding share of 3.1% in the region's general bond market. In Q2 2025, LCY financing accounted for 75.6% of the region's sustainable bond issuance, which was lower than the corresponding shares of 95.0% in its general bond market and 88.9% in the EU-20's sustainable bond market. In Q2 2025, 82.9% of ASEAN+3 sustainable bond issuance carried maturities of less than 5 years, resulting in a size-weighted average maturity of 5.1 years. In ASEAN markets, LCY financing comprised 99.5% of sustainable bond issuance during the quarter, while bonds with maturities over 5 years accounted for 61.3% of total issuance, driven by longer-term government borrowing. ASEAN sustainable bond issuance in Q2 2025 recorded a size-weighted average maturity of 13.9 years, exceeding the EU-20's 8.5 years. In ASEAN, 60.8% of sustainable bond financing originated in the public sector in Q2 2025, compared with 28.2% in ASEAN+3. A special section in this issue of the *Asia Bond Monitor* documents how sovereign sustainable bond issuances help improve liquidity and reduce yield spreads for corporate sustainable bonds, as sovereign issuances improve supply and demand conditions in sustainable bond markets.

[2] ASEAN+3 comprises the member states of the Association of Southeast Asian Nations (ASEAN) plus the People's Republic of China; Hong Kong, China; Japan; and the Republic of Korea.

Developments in Regional Financial Conditions

Emerging East Asian financial conditions improved between 2 June and 29 August over continued monetary easing in the region.[1] Increased expectations of a United States (US) Federal Reserve (Fed) pivot added further impetus. Progress on several trade deals in the region as well as a truce in trade negotiations between the People's Republic of China (PRC) and the US helped mollify investor concerns. During the review period, narrowed risk premiums, gains in equity markets, net portfolio equity inflows, and lower local currency (LCY) bond yields were seen in most emerging East Asian markets (**Table A**). Regional currencies were largely stable, recording a marginal appreciation on a gross domestic product (GDP)-weighted average basis. Risks to regional financial conditions are balanced. While regional central banks signaled their scope for further monetary easing to support growth amid a clouded global outlook, downside risks remain over continued uncertainty related to trade policies, the US monetary policy path, and geopolitical factors.

Bond yield movements diverged in major advanced economies during the review period. In the US, both 2-year and 10-year bond yields declined over rising expectations of a Fed rate cut following weak labor market data released in early August. On the other hand, bond yields rose in the euro area over the "wait-and-watch" stance adopted by the European Central Bank (ECB) and in Japan over improving economic performance and still-elevated inflation.

The 2-year and 10-year US yields declined during the review period as weaker labor market data raised the prospect of faster-than-expected Fed easing. The US

Table A: Changes in Financial Conditions in Major Advanced Economies and Select Emerging East Asian Markets from 2 June to 29 August 2025

	2-Year Government Bond Yield (bps)	10-Year Government Bond Yield (bps)	5-Year Credit Default Swap Spread (bps)	Equity Index (%)	FX Rate (%)
Major Advanced Economies					
Euro Area	15	20	–	(0.1)	2.1
Japan	10	9	(2.7)	9.9	(3.0)
United States	(32)	(21)	–	8.8	–
Select Emerging East Asian Markets					
People's Republic of China	(6)	8	(8.0)	15.2	1.0
Hong Kong, China	47	(5)	–	8.3	0.6
Indonesia	(85)	(44)	(9.1)	10.8	(1.5)
Republic of Korea	2	2	(8.9)	18.0	(0.8)
Malaysia	(14)	(14)	(9.8)	4.4	0.8
Philippines	(9)	(26)	(2.4)	(3.1)	(2.5)
Singapore	(52)	(59)	–	9.7	0.1
Thailand	(41)	(49)	(10.6)	7.6	1.3
Viet Nam	51	44	(16.8)	25.9	(1.2)

( ) = negative, – = not available, bps = basis points, FX = foreign exchange.

Note: FX rates are presented against the United States dollar. A positive (negative) value for the FX rate indicates the appreciation (depreciation) of the local currency against the United States dollar.

Source: *AsianBondsOnline* calculations based on Bloomberg LP data.

[1] Emerging East Asia is defined to include member states of the Association of Southeast Asian Nations plus the People's Republic of China; Hong Kong, China; and the Republic of Korea.

economy showed some improvement during the review period, albeit with emerging signs of weakness. While annualized GDP growth rebounded to an upwardly revised 3.3% in the second quarter (Q2) of 2025 from a contraction of 0.5% in the prior quarter, annualized GDP growth in the first half of 2025 averaged only 1.4% versus 2.3% in the same period a year earlier. In June, the Fed revised its 2025 GDP growth forecast downward to 1.4% from an estimate of 1.7% in March and reduced its 2026 projection to 1.6% from 1.8%. Retail sales growth rebounded to 0.5% month-on-month (m-o-m) in July and 0.9% m-o-m in June from a 0.8% m-o-m contraction in May. The S&P Global US Manufacturing Purchasing Managers Index (PMI) strengthened to 53.0 in August from 49.8 in July and 52.9 in June. However, industrial production posted a marginal contraction of 0.1% m-o-m in July after gaining 0.4% m-o-m in June and 0.1% m-o-m in May. Moreover, recent data on nonfarm payroll employment suggest that labor market growth was weaker than previously understood. Nonfarm payroll employment posted additions of 22,000 in August, well below the expected gain of 75,000 and July's revised figure of 79,000. The July nonfarm payroll employment additions were also well below the expected 105,000. More significantly, the new jobs figure for June was revised downward in July to 14,000 from 147,000; in August it was further revised to reflect a net loss of 13,000 jobs in June. The unemployment rate also ticked up during the review period, reaching 4.3% in August from 4.2% in July and 4.1% in June. The weakened employment figures prompted a reassessment of the current state of the US economy, raising expectations of a rate cut at the Fed's September meeting. On 2 June, CME FedWatch's probability of a 25 basis points (bps) rate cut in September stood at 54.2%, rising to 86.4% on 29 August and 91.1% on 10 September.

Inflation in the US rose during the review period and remained above the 2.0% target. Consumer price inflation ticked up to 2.9% year-on-year (y-o-y) in August and 2.7% y-o-y in July and June, compared to 2.4% y-o-y in May and 2.3% y-o-y in April. Core inflation rose to 3.1% y-o-y in August and July, and 2.9% y-o-y in June, up from 2.8% y-o-y in May. Personal Consumption Expenditures (PCE) inflation also climbed to 2.6% y-o-y in July and June from 2.4% y-o-y in May. Core PCE inflation inched up to 2.9% y-o-y in July from 2.8% y-o-y in June and May. In its June forecasts, the Fed revised upward its PCE forecasts for 2025 and 2026 to 3.0% y-o-y and 2.4% y-o-y, respectively, from forecasts of 2.7% y-o-y and 2.2% y-o-y made in March. Core PCE inflation projections for 2025 and 2026 were also revised upward to 3.1% y-o-y and 2.4% y-o-y, respectively, from 2.8% y-o-y and 2.2% y-o-y. The Fed believes that the full effects of tariffs have yet to be reflected in consumer prices.[2] Meanwhile, the impacts of tariffs were being seen in producer prices in July, with producer price inflation rising to 3.3% y-o-y from 2.4% y-o-y in June. Core producer price inflation rose to 3.7% y-o-y in July from 2.6% y-o-y in June. On a m-o-m basis, producer prices rose 0.9% in July, the fastest increase since March 2022. Also reflecting tariff pressures, import prices rose 0.4% m-o-m in July following declines of 0.1% m-o-m in June and 0.4% m-o-m in May.

Market expectations of the future US monetary policy stance reversed several times during the review period, ending with a more dovish outlook by 29 August. The shifts were mirrored in the data from CME FedWatch (**Figure A**).

- **Phase A:** Amid concerns over the impacts of tariffs on inflation and growth, the Fed left unchanged the federal funds target rate range at 4.25%–4.50% during its 17–18 June Federal Open Market Committee (FOMC) meeting, noting that while the economy continues to expand, inflation remains elevated.[3] The June FOMC meeting affirmed the March projection of two rate cuts (totaling 50 bps)

Figure A: Daily Probability of Cumulative Rate Adjustments by the Federal Reserve in 2025

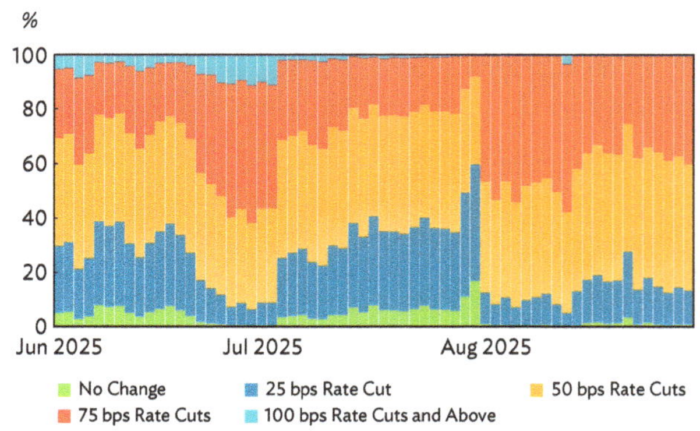

bps = basis points.
Note: Data are as of 29 August 2025.
Source: CME FedWatch Tool.

2 US Federal Reserve, Federal Open Market Committee. 2025. Minutes of the Federal Open Market Committee of 29–30 July 2025.

3 US Federal Reserve. 2025. Federal Reserve Issues FOMC Statement. Press release. 18 June.

in 2025. On 20 June, the likelihood of a cumulative 75 bps rate cut in 2025 was 27.3% per CME FedWatch.

- **Phase B:** Despite the wait-and-see stance exhibited at the June FOMC meeting, there were some investor expectations of a rate cut at the subsequent July FOMC meeting. On 20 June, Fed Governor Christopher Waller expressed his view that the impact of tariffs on inflation would be minimal and that the Fed should cut rates in July. On 23 June, Fed Vice Chair for Supervision Michelle Bowman stated that she also favored a rate cut in July if inflationary pressures were low. During the Semiannual Banking Committee Testimony on 24 June, Fed Chair Jerome Powell said that it would be possible for the Fed to cut rates in July if inflation fell. On 30 June, the likelihood of a cumulative 75 bps rate cut in 2025 rose to 50.5%.
- **Phase C:** Expectations of a July rate cut were dampened in early July. On 1 July, Fed Chair Jerome Powell highlighted that they were largely in a wait-and-see mode over the imposition of US tariffs. He indicated that the Fed would have already cut rates if not for the uncertainty brought about by tariff policies. In addition, the stronger-than-expected June nonfarm payroll data released on 3 July—147,000 additions compared to an expected 106,000—further bolstered the likelihood of the Fed holding rates steady at its July meeting. The likelihood of a cumulative 75 bps rate cut in 2025 fell to 29.6% on 3 July, with a hawkish stance being backed by several Fed members throughout July.[4] As widely expected, the federal funds target rate range was held unchanged during the 29–30 July FOMC meeting as the Fed considered the impact of economic growth moderation in the first half of 2025.[5]
- **Phase D:** Following the weak July nonfarm payroll data released on 1 August, a few Fed officials turned dovish.[6] The probability of a cumulative 75 bps rate cut in 2025 rose to 53.1% on 4 August. However, the release of rising Producer Price Index data on 15 August reignited inflationary concerns, pushing down the probability of a cumulative 75 bps rate in 2025 to 36.0% on the same day.[7] This probability dipped all the way to 25.4% on 21 August after the release of the Fed's July minutes showing that members judged inflationary risks to be more serious than labor market concerns. However, the probability rose again to 40.1% on 29 August, following the Jackson Hole symposium on 21–23 August when Fed Chair Jerome Powell acknowledged a challenging situation with risks to both labor markets and inflation, indicating that an adjustment in policy was warranted given the shifting balance of risks.

The euro area witnessed rising bond yields during the review period amid the ECB's wait-and-see policy stance and stable economic growth. GDP growth eased slightly to 1.5% y-o-y in Q2 2025 from 1.6% y-o-y in the first quarter (Q1) of 2025, while still exceeding the 1.3% y-o-y growth recorded in the fourth quarter of 2024. In August, the euro area's manufacturing PMI continued to trend upward and into expansionary territory (i.e., above the 50-point threshold) to 50.7 after reaching 49.8 in July, 49.5 in June, and 49.4 in May. The unemployment rate fell slightly to 6.2% in July from 6.3% in June and 6.4% in May. Inflation remained largely in line with the ECB's expectations and target, with some upward pressure amid global trade uncertainty. The y-o-y inflation rate inched up to 2.1% in August from 2.0% in July and June. With inflation hovering around the 2.0% target, the ECB held its policy rates steady at its 24 July meeting, noting that economic growth and inflation were evolving as expected.[8] ECB officials highlighted that the inflation outlook is related to the external trade environment.[9] Some ECB officials consistently reiterated the ECB's wait-and-watch stance after the meeting.[10]

4 On 2 July, Fed Bank of Richmond President Thomas Barkin noted there was no urgency to lower rates. On 3 July, Fed Bank of Atlanta President Raphael Bostic cited that a wait-and-see approach could help given uncertainty. On 15 July, Fed Bank of Dallas President Lorrie Logan indicated that it was necessary to hold rates steady to help cool inflation but the Fed might also need to pivot if inflation and the labor market softened.

5 US Federal Reserve. 2025. Decisions Regarding Monetary Policy Implementation. Press release. 30 July.

6 For example, on 4 August, Fed Bank of San Franciso President Mary Daly noted that an imminent rate cut was possible given the labor data. On 6 August, Fed Bank of Minneapolis President Neel Kashkari indicated that the Fed might cut interest rates soon. On the same day, Fed Governor Lisa Cook highlighted that the labor data were consistent with turning points in the economy. On 10 August, Fed Vice Chair for Supervision Michelle Bowman announced she expected three rate cuts in 2025 given the weak labor data.

7 Fed Bank of Chicago President Austan Goolsbee indicated that recent inflation data and uncertainties over tariffs made him hesitant to lower rates.

8 ECB. 2025. Monetary Policy Statement of Christine Lagarde, President of the ECB. Press release. 24 July.

9 ECB. 2025. Monetary Policy Press Conference, President of the ECB. Press release. 24 July.

10 On 25 July, Bank of Latvia Governor Martins Kazaks and Deutsche Bundesbank President Joachim Nagel both indicated that there is value in holding current rates steady. On 26 July, ECB Governing Member Piero Cipollone explained that in September (and afterward) they would have more information to better make their assessment. On 29 July, Central Bank of Ireland Governor Gabriel Makhlouf mentioned that they have reached a point where they can "wait and see." On 6 August, Oesterreichische Nationalbank Governor Robert Holzmann expressed that the ECB should "wait and see" what economic developments arise.

In Japan, both 2-year and 10-year bond yields rose during the review period, driven by strengthened economic performance and still-elevated inflation. Government bond yields fell in June, as the government reduced the amount of government bonds to be auctioned, and rose in July and August on uncertainty over the results of the House of Councilors election on 20 July and the release of stronger-than-expected economic data in the first half of August. Japan's GDP grew 2.2% y-o-y in Q2 2025 versus an expected 1.0% y-o-y and compared with 0.6% y-o-y in Q1 2025. However, y-o-y growth in both quarters was down from the economy's 2.4% y-o-y expansion in Q4 2024. Industrial production contracted 0.9% y-o-y in July after gaining 4.4% y-o-y in June, but this was still better than May's 2.4% y-o-y decline. Manufacturing PMI stood at 49.7 in August and 48.9 in July yet remained below June's 50.1. At its 30–31 July meeting, the Bank of Japan (BOJ) revised upward its 2025 GDP growth forecast to 0.6% y-o-y from its 0.5% y-o-y estimate in April. Japan's inflation has been trending down but remains above the BOJ's target. Consumer price inflation fell slightly to 3.1% y-o-y in July from 3.3% y-o-y in June and 3.5% y-o-y in May. The BOJ revised its 2025 inflation forecast to 2.7% in July from 2.2% in April. Despite upgrading its economic forecasts, the BOJ kept the policy rate unchanged at its 16–17 June and 30–31 July monetary policy meetings, noting the uncertain impact of global trade policies on the economy.

Both 2-year and 10-year bond yields fell in most emerging East Asian markets between 2 June and 29 August amid continued disinflationary progress and monetary easing by some regional central banks, as well as increased expectations of a Fed rate cut in September (**Table B**). Most regional markets witnessed either lower or stable inflation during the review period (**Figure B**). For example, in Indonesia, although inflation rose to 2.3% y-o-y in August and 2.4% y-o-y in July from 1.9% y-o-y in June, it remained well within the target range of 1.5%–3.5%. Four central banks in Southeast Asia eased monetary policy to support growth during the review period, while other regional central banks pursued a wait-and-see stance. Bangko Sentral ng Pilipinas cut its policy rate by 25 bps on 19 June and again on 28 August, citing moderating inflation, global uncertainties, and the need to support growth. On 9 July, Bank Negara Malaysia cut its policy rate by 25 bps as a preemptive action in anticipation of the potential impact of external uncertainties. Bank Indonesia conducted successive 25 bps rate cuts during its 15–16 July and 19–20 August meetings, marking its third and fourth rate cuts for the year, respectively. On 13 August, the

Table B: Changes in Monetary Stances in Major Advanced Economies and Select Emerging East Asian Markets

Economy	Policy Rate 1-Aug-2024 (%)	Rate Change (%) Aug-2024	Sep-2024	Oct-2024	Nov-2024	Dec-2024	Jan-2025	Feb-2025	Mar-2025	Apr-2025	May-2025	Jun-2025	Jul-2025	Aug-2025	Policy Rate 29-Aug-2025 (%)	Change in Policy Rates (basis points)
Euro Area	3.75		↓0.25	↓0.25		↓0.25		↓0.25	↓0.25	↓0.25		↓0.25			2.00	↓ 175
Japan	0.25						↑0.25								0.50	↑ 25
United Kingdom	5.00				↓0.25			↓0.25			↓0.25			↓0.25	4.00	↓ 100
United States	5.50		↓0.50		↓0.25	↓0.25									4.50	↓ 100
People's Republic of China	1.70		↓0.20								↓0.10				1.40	↓ 30
Indonesia	6.25		↓0.25				↓0.25				↓0.25		↓0.25	↓0.25	5.00	↓ 125
Republic of Korea	3.50			↓0.25	↓0.25			↓0.25			↓0.25				2.50	↓ 100
Malaysia	3.00												↓0.25		2.75	↓ 25
Philippines	6.50	↓0.25		↓0.25		↓0.25				↓0.25		↓0.25		↓0.25	5.00	↓ 150
Singapore	–						↓			↓					–	↓ –
Thailand	2.50			↓0.25				↓0.25		↓0.25				↓0.25	1.50	↓ 100
Viet Nam	4.50														4.50	◆ 0

( ) = negative, – = no data.

Notes:

1. Data coverage is from 1 August 2024 to 29 August 2025.
2. For the People's Republic of China, the data used in the chart are for the 7-day reverse repurchase rate.
3. For the United States, the upper bound of the policy rate target range is reported on the table.
4. An arrow up (down) indicates a policy rate hike (cut). A diamond indicates no change in the policy rate.
5. The up (down) arrow for Singapore signifies monetary policy tightening (loosening) by its central bank. The Monetary Authority of Singapore utilizes the Singapore dollar nominal effective exchange rate to guide its monetary policy.

Sources: Various central bank websites.

Figure B: Inflation in Major Advanced Economies and Select Emerging East Asian Markets

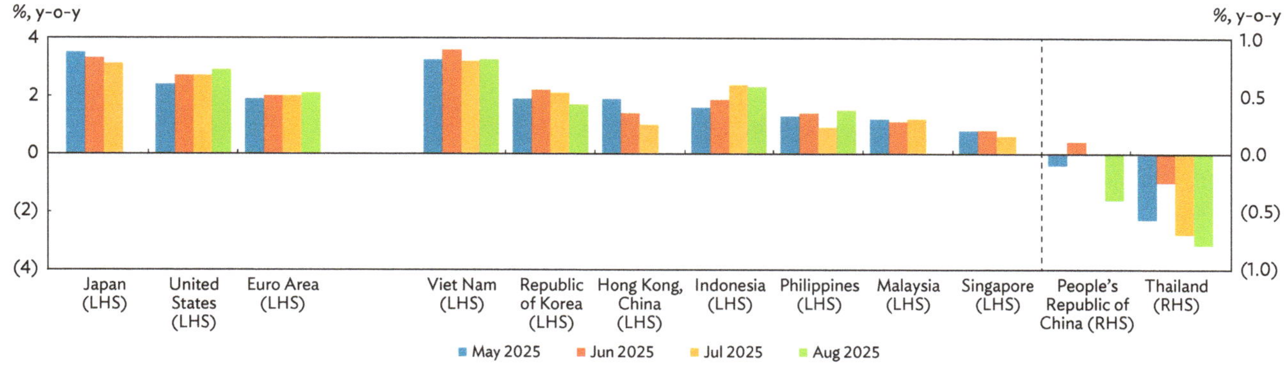

( ) = negative, LHS = left-hand side, RHS = right-hand side, y-o-y = year-on-year.

Notes:

1. For Hong Kong, China; Japan; Malaysia; and Singapore, data are up to July 2025.
2. For the People's Republic of China, July 2025 inflation was at 0.0% year-on-year. For the euro area, August 2025 data is based on preliminary estimate.

Sources: Various local sources.

Bank of Thailand reduced its policy rate by 25 bps over subdued inflation and to support the economy amid the impact of tariffs. Focus Economics' August forecast showed that moderating inflation and tariff uncertainties led to increased expectations of further easing by most Southeast Asian central banks before the end of the year, compared with June's forecast (**Figure C**). For example, in July, Bank Indonesia indicated that it would consider cutting interest rates further amid a tame inflation outlook and a weak global economy. On 11 August, Bangko Sentral ng Pilipinas Governor Eli Remolona mentioned that two more rate cuts within the year were likely.

Figure C: Current Policy Rates and End-2025 Projections in Select Emerging East Asian Economies

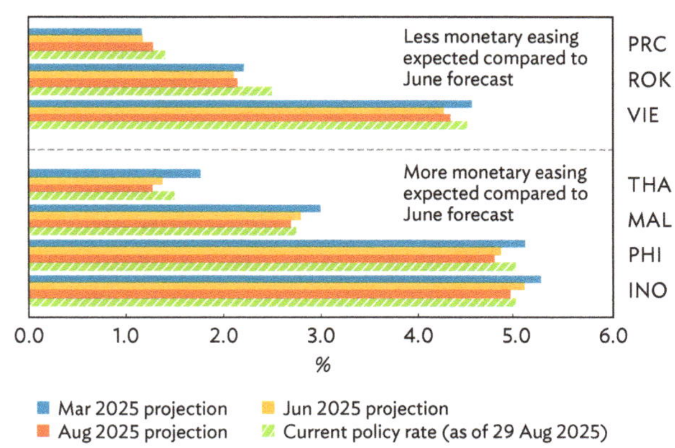

PRC = People's Republic of China; INO = Indonesia; ROK = Republic of Korea; MAL = Malaysia; PHI = Philippines; THA = Thailand; VIE = Viet Nam.

Sources: Various central banks and Focus Economics projections.

Amid ongoing monetary easing and disinflation during the review period, emerging East Asian bond markets witnessed an average decline of 12 bps and 16 bps in 2-year and 10-year bond yields, respectively. Across the region, Viet Nam saw increases of 51 bps and 44 bps in its respective 2-year and 10-year yields, driven by strong domestic economic growth (the highest in the region) and relatively high inflation (also the highest in the region) despite a decline in inflation in July. To reach its 2025 growth target of 8.3%–8.5%, the Government of Viet Nam implemented several fiscal measures such as implementing a 2 percentage point reduction in the value-added tax, which is expected to raise the fiscal deficit and increase government bond issuance. In the Republic of Korea, 2-year and 10-year bond yields rose marginally by 2 bps each as the Bank of Korea held its base rate steady at its 28 August and 10 July meetings amid uncertainty in the domestic outlook. On 28 August, the Bank of Korea noted that while domestic growth has improved, uncertainty remains high over tariffs. As a result of the Bank of Korea's cautious comments, investors expected less easing, as reflected in Figure C. During the review period, the PRC's 10-year yield saw an increase of 8 bps as the People's Bank of China signaled in its August monetary report that there was no urgency to cut rates.

Despite lingering trade policy uncertainty, many regional economies recorded faster GDP growth in Q2 2025 than in Q1 2025 (**Table C**). Viet Nam remained the fastest-growing economy in the region with GDP growth

Table C: Gross Domestic Product Growth in Select Emerging East Asian Economies (y-o-y, %)

Economy	2025 Q1	2025 Q2	Forecast for 2025
PRC	5.40	5.20	4.70
HKG	3.00	3.10	2.00
INO	4.87	5.12	5.00
ROK	0.00	0.60	0.80
MAL	4.40	4.40	4.30
PHI	5.40	5.50	5.60
SIN	4.10	4.40	1.60
THA	3.20	2.80	1.80
VIE	6.93	7.96	6.30

PRC = People's Republic of China; HKG = Hong Kong, China; INO = Indonesia; ROK = Republic of Korea; MAL = Malaysia; PHI = Philippines; Q1 = first quarter; Q2 = second quarter; SIN = Singapore; THA = Thailand; VIE = Viet Nam; y-o-y = year-on-year.

Note: Forecasts for 2025 are based on the *Asian Development Outlook July 2025*.

Sources: Various local sources.

Figure D: Changes in Credit Default Swap Spreads in Select Emerging East Asian Markets (senior 5-year)

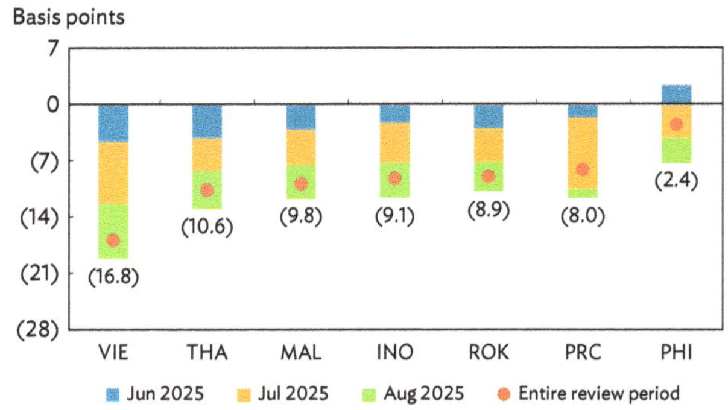

( ) = negative; PRC = People's Republic of China; INO = Indonesia; ROK = Republic of Korea; MAL = Malaysia; PHI = Philippines; THA = Thailand; VIE = Viet Nam.

Note: The numbers above (below) each bar refer to the change in spreads between 2 June 2025 and 29 August 2025.

Source: *AsianBondsOnline* calculations based on Bloomberg LP data.

accelerating to 8.0% y-o-y in Q2 2025 from 6.9% y-o-y in the previous quarter, supported by growth across all major sectors, led by manufacturing and construction and services. GDP growth also ticked up during the review period in the Republic of Korea to 0.6% y-o-y from 0.0% y-o-y due to improvements in domestic consumption (1.4% y-o-y versus 1.0% y-o-y) and export growth (4.5% y-o-y versus 1.5% y-o-y). In Indonesia, GDP growth accelerated to 5.1% y-o-y in Q2 2025 from 4.9% y-o-y in Q1 2025, with expansions recorded across all expenditure components except government spending. GDP growth in Singapore reached 4.4% y-o-y in Q2 2025, exceeding both the advance estimate of 4.3% y-o-y and the 4.1% y-o-y growth in Q1 2025, with faster growth recorded in both the goods and services sectors. With strong growth in the first half of the year, the government revised Singapore's 2025 growth forecast upward to 1.5%–2.5% from an earlier estimate of 0.0%–2.0%. Economic growth in the PRC reached 5.2% y-o-y in Q2 2025, compared with expected growth of 5.1% y-o-y and Q1 2025's expansion of 5.4% y-o-y, which was partly boosted by government support measures amid tariff policy uncertainties. Meanwhile, Thailand's GDP growth slowed to 2.8% y-o-y in Q2 2025 from 3.2% y-o-y in Q1 2025 due to a deceleration in the growth of exports and investments.

Despite uncertainty in the external environment, financial conditions improved in the region during the review period. Besides continued monetary easing, the improvement was supported by progress in tariff negotiations and the expectations of a US rate cut in September. Risk premiums, as measured by credit default swap (CDS) spreads, collectively narrowed during the review period across regional markets. From 2 June to 29 August, the region's average CDS spread narrowed by 9.4 bps from 59.7 bps to 50.3 bps (simple average) and by 8.3 bps from 52.9 bps to 44.6 bps (GDP-weighted). As shown in **Figure D**, in June, risk premiums declined due to the Israel–Iran ceasefire, while in July and August, investor sentiment was buoyed by a slew of tariff agreements and an extension on the tariff pause between the PRC and the US. During the review period, the CDS spread fell the most in Viet Nam (–16.8 bps) as it was the first market in the region that closed a trade agreement with the US in early July. On the other hand, there was a rise in the CDS spread in the Philippines in June amid political concerns surrounding the vice-president's impeachment as well as rising debt levels.

Improved investor sentiment was also evident in strong equity market performances in regional markets. Most regional equity markets recorded gains in July, as various trade deals eased tariff tensions, and in August on expectations of a September Fed rate cut (**Figure E**). During the review period, the region's equity markets gained 10.8% (simple-average) and 13.0% (market-weighted). The largest equity gains occurred in Viet Nam where investor optimism over strong GDP growth and stock market reforms contributed to a 25.9% increase. This was followed by the Republic of Korea with a gain of 18.0% on easing political concerns and optimism over

Figure E: Changes in Equity Indexes in Select Emerging East Asian Markets

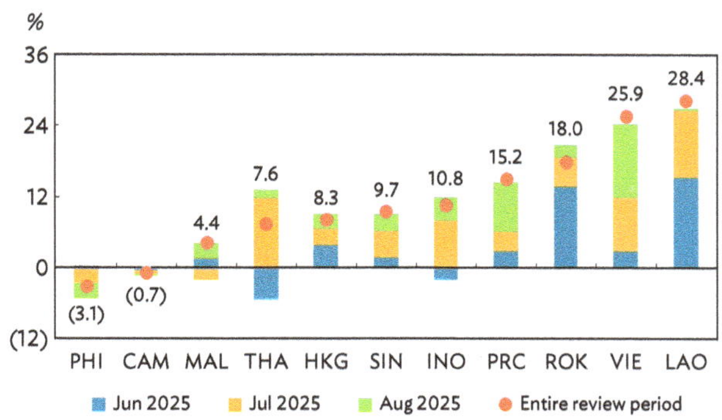

( ) = negative; CAM = Cambodia; PRC = People's Republic of China; HKG = Hong Kong, China; INO = Indonesia; ROK = Republic of Korea; LAO = Lao People's Democratic Republic; MAL = Malaysia; PHI = Philippines; SIN = Singapore; THA = Thailand; VIE = Viet Nam.

Note: The numbers above (below) each bar refer to the percentage change between 2 June 2025 and 29 August 2025.

Source: *AsianBondsOnline* calculations based on Bloomberg LP data.

Figure F: Foreign Capital Flows in Select Emerging East Asian Equity Markets

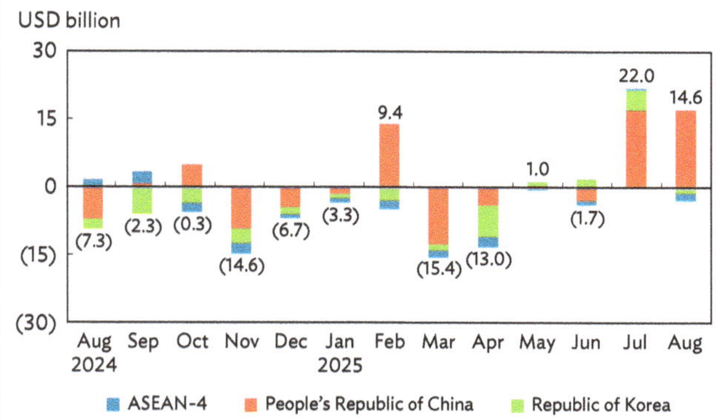

( ) = outflows, USD = United States dollar.

Notes:

1. Data coverage is from 1 August 2024 to 29 August 2025.
2. The numbers above (below) each bar refer to net inflows (net outflows) for each month.
3. Emerging East Asia is defined to include member states of the Association of Southeast Asian Nations (ASEAN) plus the People's Republic of China; Hong Kong, China; and the Republic of Korea.
4. ASEAN-4 includes Indonesia, the Philippines, Thailand, and Viet Nam.

Source: Institute of International Finance.

corporate governance reforms. Similarly, the PRC's equity market gained 15.2% during the review period amid higher-than-expected GDP growth in Q2 2025, stock market reforms, and monetary easing measures. In April and May, the People's Bank of China released CNY600 billion (USD82.3 billion) via the medium-term lending facility and cut the reserve requirement ratio and 7-day reverse repo rate. In addition, stock market reforms were announced on 7 May to (i) encourage listed companies to improve corporate governance, (ii) consolidate an existing market stabilization fund, (iii) expand a pilot investment program for insurance companies, (iv) release an action plan to strengthen the mutual fund industry, and (v) reduce risk weightings for stock market investments by insurance companies. Only the Philippines posted equity market losses (–3.1%) during the review period; investor sentiment was dampened by the weakening growth outlook as the government lowered its growth forecast for the year and amid concerns over rising debt levels.

Emerging East Asia's strong equity market performance was partly supported by net equity capital inflows. Between 2 June and 29 August, the region posted net portfolio inflows into equity markets of USD35.0 billion, supported by easing tariff concerns and market-specific factors (**Figure F**). In June, there were net portfolio equity outflows of USD1.7 billion as the US' initial tariff pause ended and uncertainty over the wider conflict in the Midde East escalated. Emerging East Asia recorded large inflows of USD22.0 billion in July on the signing of several trade agreements as well as on progress in trade talks between the US and other trading partners. The PRC posted net portfolio inflows of USD17.3 billion in July over better-than-expected GDP figures. In August, the region posted net inflows of USD14.6 billion, largely driven by the PRC (USD17.3 billion) following the extension of the PRC–US tariff pause and news benefiting its technology sector. Specifically, DeepSeek updated its artificial intelligence model, further boosting market sentiment. In addition, the government asked local technology firms to focus on buying from local chipmakers instead of from foreign companies. Viet Nam posted the region's largest outflows (USD1.5 billion) in August, largely driven by the portfolio rebalancing of some international investors. At the same time, the equity market was well supported by domestic investors amid ongoing stock market reforms, such as the establishment of a central counterparty clearing system, and strong economic growth in the first half of 2025, which led to solid gains in Viet Nam's equity market during the review period.

During June–July, the region's bond markets recorded net portfolio outflows of USD9.4 billion, driven by market-specific factors (**Figure G**). The largest bond outflows came from the PRC (USD11.9 billion), largely due to a shift in investments from bonds to equities amid a domestic stock market boom. On the other hand, the Republic of Korea witnessed net bond inflows of

Figure G: Foreign Capital Flows in Select Emerging East Asian Local Currency Bond Markets

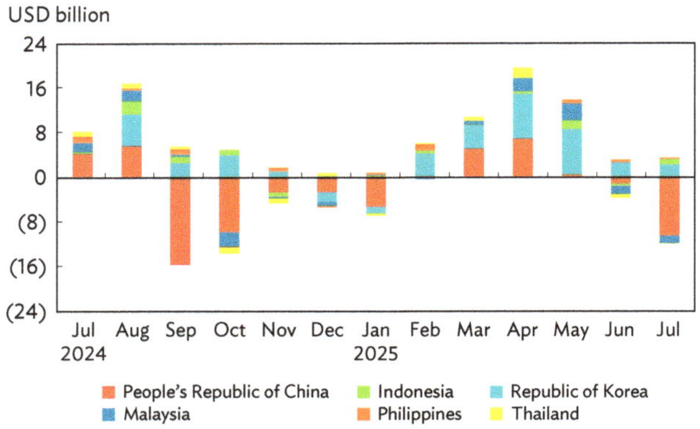

( ) = negative, USD = United States dollar.

Notes:
1. The Republic of Korea and Thailand provided data on bond flows. For the People's Republic of China, Indonesia, Malaysia, and the Philippines, month-on-month changes in foreign holdings of local currency government bonds were used as a proxy for bond flows.
2. Data are as of 31 July 2025.
3. Figures were computed based on 31 July 2025 exchange rates and do not include currency effects.

Sources: People's Republic of China (Bloomberg LP); Indonesia (Directorate General of Budget Financing and Risk Management, Ministry of Finance); Republic of Korea (Financial Supervisory Service); Malaysia (Bank Negara Malaysia); Philippines (Bureau of the Treasury); and Thailand (Thai Bond Market Association).

USD4.8 billion due to improved investment sentiment as political concerns eased following the presidential elections and indications that the Bank of Korea would keep rates elevated. The Philippines recorded inflows of USD0.6 billion in June–July amid speculation that its market would be included in JP Morgan's EM bond index. Indonesia also recorded bond inflows of USD0.6 billion during the period as investors shifted from Bank Indonesia Rupiah Securities to Treasury bonds following a reduction in issuance of the former by the central bank.

Emerging East Asian currencies were largely stable during the review period, supported by sound economic growth and improved investment sentiment. The region saw a 0.2% simple-average currency depreciation against the US dollar but an appreciation of 0.6% on a GDP-weighted average basis. The Philippine peso saw the largest depreciation across the region at 2.5%, driven by two rate cuts during the review period and heightened concerns regarding the current account deficit (**Figure H**). On 13 June, the Philippines revealed it had recorded a current account deficit of USD4.2 billion in Q1 2025, doubling the USD2.1 billion tallied in the same period a year earlier. The government also revised downward its 2025 economic growth target to 5.5%–6.5% on 26 June

Figure H: Currency Exchange Rates Against the United States Dollar in Select Emerging East Asian Markets

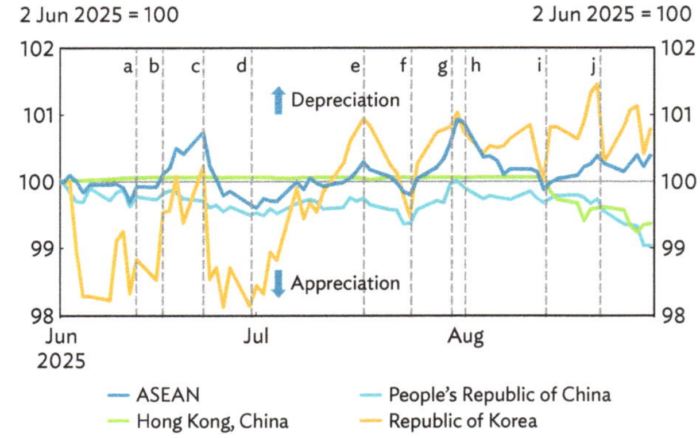

ASEAN = Association of Southeast Asian Nations, US = United States.

Notes:
1. Corresponding dates of the following events:
   a Israel attacks Iran's nuclear facilities.
   b The Fed maintains the federal funds rate at a range of 4.25%–4.50% at the June FOMC meeting.
   c Israel–Iran ceasefire announced.
   d US consumer spending fell in May, dampening global growth prospects.
   e Fed Governor Christopher Waller advocates for a rate cut.
   f Fed Chair Jerome Powell advocates a wait-and-see stance on the federal fund target rate.
   g The Fed keeps the federal funds rate unchanged at a range of 4.25%–4.50% at the July FOMC meeting.
   h Announcement of weaker-than-expected nonfarm payroll additions in July.
   i Some Fed officials express hesitation about cutting rates at the September FOMC meeting.
   j Start of the Fed's Jackson Hole Symposium.
2. ASEAN comprises the markets of Brunei Darussalam, Cambodia, Indonesia, the Lao People's Democratic Republic, Malaysia, the Philippines, Singapore, Thailand, and Viet Nam.
3. Data are as of 29 August 2025.
4. An increase (decrease) in the value indicates depreciation (appreciation) of the currency against the US dollar.

Source: *AsianBondsOnline* calculations based on Bloomberg LP data.

from 6.0%–8.0% in December 2024. The second-largest depreciation was observed in Indonesia (1.5%), following two consecutive 25 bps rate cuts in July and August. The Vietnamese dong also weakened by 1.2% following government directives to keep interest rates low, which led to increased demand for US dollars from financial institutions and domestic investors.

Risks to the outlook for regional financial conditions are balanced. On the upside, regional central banks signaled scope for further monetary easing to support growth. Downside risks mostly come from external sources, including uncertainties over US trade and monetary policies, as well as geopolitical tensions:

- Trade policy uncertainty continues to weigh heavily on investor confidence. Although markets reacted positively to the 90-day extension of the PRC–US trade truce, the potential scale and timing of tariffs remain unpredictable, which could trigger renewed market volatility. According to the *Asian Development Outlook July 2025*, higher tariffs and/or a re-escalation of PRC–US trade tensions could reduce regional growth, with most of the impact expected in 2026. Meanwhile, an escalation of the PRC–US tariff dispute would push inflation higher in the US and lower in most regional economies (except the PRC) due to weaker global demand. In addition to the overall tariffs imposed on economies, sector-specific tariffs add another layer of uncertainty. Continued uncertainty in trade policies could erode investment sentiment, curtail global and regional investment activity, and slow economic growth. Moreover, growing concerns about a more fragmented global economy may undermine international cooperation, disrupt cross-border capital flows, weaken the global financial safety net, and heighten systemic financial vulnerabilities.

- US monetary policy uncertainty beyond the expected September rate cut also contributes to risks to the region's financial conditions. Tariff-related price pressures could spread beyond a temporary adjustment and become embedded in broader cost structures, particularly through intermediate goods. These higher input costs could ripple through the entire production chain as businesses pass them on to other producers and consumers, sustaining higher inflation over time. In addition, a sustained depreciation of the US dollar could further amplify import-driven inflation, while geopolitical tensions may intensify cost pressures and financial market volatility. Slowing growth among its major trading partners could reduce demand for US exports and tighten global liquidity, raising the likelihood of policy trade-offs in which the Fed must balance supporting growth against maintaining price stability. Such dynamics increase the risk of policy misjudgments and abrupt market repricing.
- Geopolitical risks remain significant. Unexpected wider conflict in the Middle East could disrupt supply chains, push up energy and food prices, and intensify global uncertainty.

Environmental and climate-related risks remain highly relevant and continue to pose significant downside threats to financial conditions. For example, weather disturbances brought about by Typhoon Wipha and monsoon rains affected the Philippines and the PRC during the review period, leading to agricultural and infrastructure losses. Extreme weather events can damage economic infrastructure, reduce output, and increase inflationary pressures, compounding other financial vulnerabilities. Disasters have been shown to raise borrowing costs by increasing expectations for future damages (**Box 1**).

Box 1: Getting the Timing Right—Disasters and Sovereign Debt Issuance

Climate change has supercharged the devastation from disasters triggered by natural hazards, threatening sustainable development. As temperatures and sea levels continue to rise, intense floods, storms, heat waves, and droughts now occur five times more often than in 1980. The economies most vulnerable to climate change account for much of this increase. Despite improvements in disaster risk management, economic losses continue to mount due to increased disaster frequency and the expansion of human settlement in disaster-prone areas. Some of the most damaging disasters in recent decades have been in Asia and the Pacific, which is home to two-thirds of people affected by disasters globally. Climate-change-related disasters threaten to erode the region's progress in poverty reduction and sustainable development.

The fiscal footprint of disasters risks jeopardizing debt sustainability. Disaster damages are sizable relative to gross domestic product (GDP), even if abstracting from indirect effects (e.g., lost tax revenue from declining economic activity) (**Figure B1.1**). The costs associated with damage from disasters have been shown to lower tax revenue and raise expenditures, budget deficits, and debt-to-GDP ratios (Acevedo 2014; Jones, Keen, and Strand 2013; Lis and Nickel 2010; Melecky and Raddatz 2011). Expectations of renewed fiscal pressures after disasters undermine sovereigns' repayment capacity, leading creditors in sovereign debt markets to ask for compensation to bear additional risks, which is known as the disaster premium. This premium adds to sovereign borrowing costs, weakening debt sustainability. Importantly, the uncertain magnitude of disaster-induced economic losses and their unpredictable timing makes self-insurance through fiscal buffers infeasible, with such buffers posing high opportunity costs.

Disasters drive up sovereign borrowing costs, but the effect fades over time. Ficarra and Raabe (forthcoming) assess the impact of disasters on borrowing costs and track the disaster premium over time. Using Bloomberg data on 2 decades of sovereign bond issuances for 112 economies mapped to records of disaster costs from EM-DAT—a disaster events database maintained by the Centre for Research on the Epidemiology of Disasters—the authors identify a significant rise in borrowing costs for post-disaster issuances. Markets attach a larger disaster premium to bonds issued shortly after disasters, with the premium fading over time. Disaster insurance further reduces the premium. Moreover, investors appear to price realized disasters more than climate change vulnerability, with effects most pronounced for floods and storms.

Figure B1.1: Disaster Damages (% of GDP)

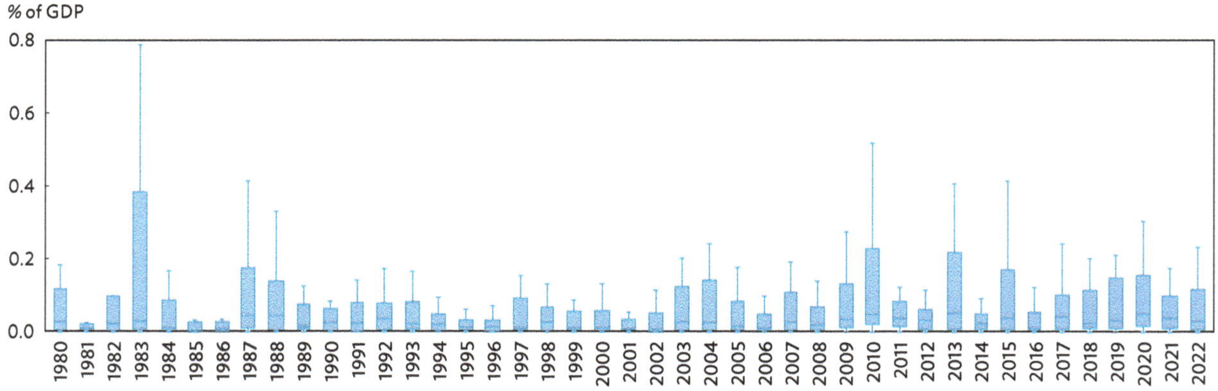

GDP = gross domestic product.

Notes: This figure exhibits for each year the cross-economy distribution of annual disaster damages as a share of GDP for economies worldwide for the period 1980–2022. The thick blue bars indicate the interquartile range.

Source: Authors' calculations based on data from EM-DAT.

This box was written by Alexander Raabe (economist) at the Asian Development Bank, Manila.

continued on next page

Box 1 *continued*

Sovereigns pay a significant disaster premium. Cumulating disaster damage costs in periods prior to bond issuance ranging from 30 days to 1 year, Ficarra and Raabe (forthcoming) find that disasters significantly raise sovereign yields and spreads (**Figure B1.2**). A 1 percentage point increase in the damages-to-GDP ratio raises borrowing costs by 29 basis points, while spreads over United States Treasuries can widen by as much 61 basis points. Based on Intergovernmental Panel on Climate Change (2021) estimates of average disaster frequency under different global warming scenarios, the disaster premium can increase borrowing costs by as much as 2.9 percentage points, a significant increase from the average 10-year yield of 3.4% prevailing in developing Asia as of July 2025.

Investors' recency bias reduces the disaster premium over time. Recency bias refers to a behavioral predisposition to attach greater importance to recent events compared to those in the past. In sovereign debt markets, this means that the disaster premium for a bond issued shortly after a disaster tends to be higher. That is, the premium declines during the time between a disaster and bond issuance. Specifically, the premium falls 2 basis points every day from the disaster to the bond issuance, translating into an average decline at the date of issuance equal to two-fifths of the initial disaster-induced increase.

Figure B1.2: Regression Coefficients of Disaster Damages on Sovereign Yields and Spreads

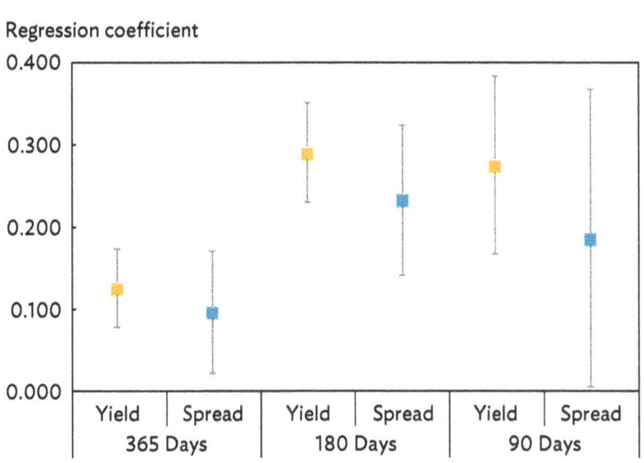

Note: This figure shows the regression coefficients of climate-change-related disaster damages on sovereign yields and spreads, controlling for bond and economy characteristics, as well as global financial conditions. Disaster damages are cumulative for 365-, 180-, and 90-day windows prior to the respective bond issuance.

Sources: Authors' calculations based on data from EM-DAT, Bloomberg, and the International Monetary Fund.

These results suggest that delaying a sovereign issuance even a few days can meaningfully reduce financing costs after a disaster.

Disasters raise borrowing costs by increasing expectations for future damages. Ficarra and Raabe (forthcoming) isolate the impact of disaster expectations by controlling for pre-disaster fundamentals affecting vulnerability and the immediate fiscal impact of disasters. This is achieved by comparing the disaster impact on bond yields at issuance to forward yields in the secondary market for bonds with the same tenor issued prior to the disaster. The results confirm an increase in borrowing costs relative to what would have been expected prior to the disaster, and thus the role of a shift in creditors' expectations.

Sovereign bond markers care more about realized disasters than vulnerability to climate change. Vulnerability to climate change has been shown to raise sovereign borrowing costs (Beirne, Renzhi, and Volz 2021; Cevik and Jalles 2022a, 2022b; International Monetary Fund 2020; Painter 2020). Going beyond mere vulnerability, Ficarra and Raabe (forthcoming) focus on realized disasters as they are more informative to expectations of future costs based on observed shifts in the probability distribution of disasters. Results from a horse race between ex ante vulnerability and ex post damage-related costs leave the latter uncontested as a driver of sovereign borrowing costs—that is, information about realized disasters is a more critical determinant of sovereign borrowing costs.

Insurance mechanisms lower the disaster premium. Drawing on EM-DAT data for disaster insurance coverage, the analysis contrasts results for insured and uninsured disasters. Results suggest that the disaster premium is lower for insured disaster damages. In contrast, uninsured damages are associated with rising borrowing costs.

The results call for mitigating elevated sovereign borrowing costs as part of post-disaster relief. Several policy conclusions apply. First, the declining disaster premium over time implies a trade-off. Sovereign debt managers are compelled to choose between elevated short-term borrowing costs for issuance right after a disaster versus waiting to issue at lower yields but at the cost of maintaining higher fiscal buffers required in the interim. Multilateral financial institutions can alleviate this trade-off by upgrading disaster financing facilities to mitigate increased post-disaster borrowing costs as part

continued on next page

Box 1 *continued*

of a relief package. Second, with climate change fueling more severe and frequent disasters, accelerating climate mitigation and adaptation is imperative to keep borrowing costs in line with debt sustainability. Finally, the results support the expansion of disaster insurance coverage—for example, by leveraging multilateral insurance facilities (e.g., catastrophe bonds).

References

S. Acevedo. 2014. Debt, Growth, and Natural Disaster: A Caribbean Trilogy. *International Monetary Fund Working Paper*. No. 14/125.

J. Beirne, N. Renzhi, and U. Volz. 2021. Feeling the Heat: Climate Risks and the Cost of Sovereign Borrowing. *International Review of Economics and Finance*. 76. 92036.

Bloomberg L.P. Government Bonds. https://www.bloomberg.com (accessed 13 December 2023).

S. Cevik and J.T. Jalles. 2022a. An Apocalypse Foretold: Climate Shocks and Sovereign Defaults. *Open Economies Review*. 33. pp. 89–108.

_____. 2022b. This Changes Everything: Climate Shocks and Sovereign Bonds. *Energy Economics*. 107. 105856.

Centre for Research on the Epidemiology of Disasters at the Université Catholique de Louvain. EM-DAT: The International Disaster Database. https://www.emdat.be/ (accessed 30 November 2023).

M. Ficarra and A. Raabe. Forthcoming. Timing the Market: When to Issue Debt After Disasters.

International Monetary Fund. 2020. The Pricing of Climate Change Physical Risks into Sovereign Bonds. *Global Financial Stability Report April 2020*.

Intergovernmental Panel on Climate Change. 2021. Summary for Policymakers. In: *Climate Change 2021: The Physical Science Basis. Contribution of Working Group I to the Sixth Assessment Report of the Intergovernmental Panel on Climate Change*, eds. V. Masson-Delmotte et al., pp. 3–32. Cambridge University Press.

B. Jones, M. Keen, and J. Strand. 2013. Fiscal Implications of Climate Change. *International Tax and Public Finance*. 20. pp. 29–70.

E. Lis and C. Nickel. The Impact of Extreme Weather Events on Budget Balances. *International Tax and Public Finance*. 17. pp. 378–399.

M. Melecky and C. Raddatz. 2011. How Do Governments Respond after Catastrophes? Natural-Disaster Shocks and the Fiscal Stance. *World Bank Policy Research Working Paper*. No. WPS 5564.

M. Painter. 2020. An Inconvenient Cost: The Effect of Climate Change on Municipal Bonds. *Journal of Financial Economics*. 135 (2). pp. 468–482.

Bond Market Developments in the Second Quarter of 2025

Section 1. Local Currency Bonds Outstanding

Local currency (LCY) bond market growth in emerging East Asia accelerated in the second quarter (Q2) of 2025 amid monetary policy easing and fiscal expansion.[11] Outstanding LCY bonds in the region reached USD28.6 trillion at the end of June on growth of 3.0% quarter-on-quarter (q-o-q), up from 2.7% q-o-q in the prior quarter (**Figure 1A**). The expansion was bolstered by the accelerated increase of corporate bonds and stable growth in government bonds. Continued monetary policy easing by most of the region's central banks in Q2 2025 supported corporate bond issuance through lower borrowing costs. Growth in the region's corporate bond segment rose to 2.1% q-o-q in Q2 2025 from 0.9% q-o-q in the first quarter (Q1), driven largely by increased issuance of corporate debt in the People's Republic of China (PRC) and the Republic of Korea following rate cuts by their respective central banks. Meanwhile, expansion in the region's stock of government bonds was stable at 3.7% q-o-q in both Q1 2025 and Q2 2025, buoyed by the continued issuance of government debt in most of the region's markets as part of fiscal policies to mitigate the impacts of global and domestic uncertainties (**Figure 1B**). At the end of June, the emerging East Asian bond market's size relative to gross domestic product had increased to 112.2% from 109.9% at the end of March but remained below the relative size of bond markets in the European Union 20 and the United States at 135.0% and 138.8%, respectively.

Figure 1: Local Currency Bonds Outstanding and Issuance

A. Bond Market Size in Select Global Markets **B. Bond Issuance in Select Emerging East Asian Markets**

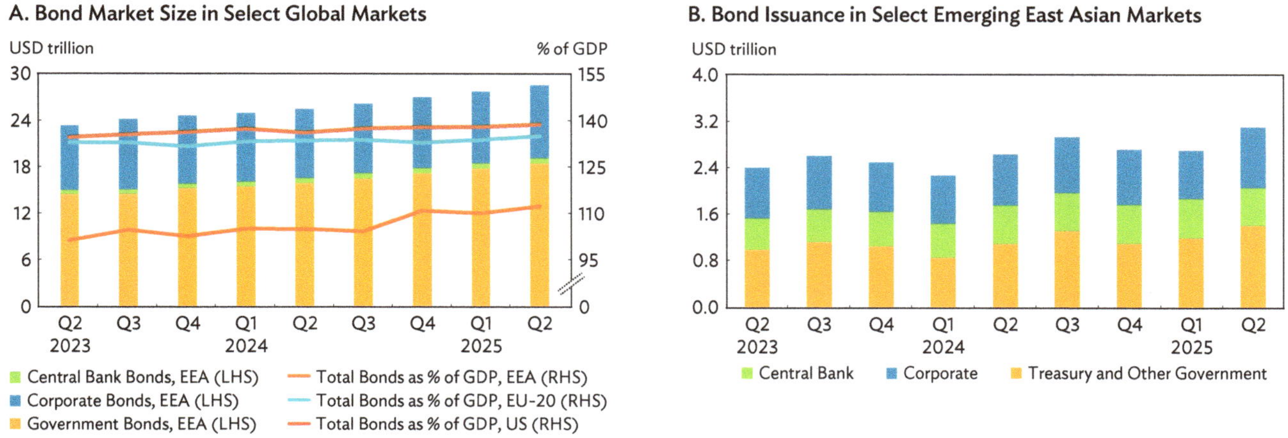

EEA = Emerging East Asia, EU- 20 = European Union 20, GDP = gross domestic product, LHS = left-hand side, RHS = right-hand side, Q1 = first quarter, Q2 = second quarter, Q3 = third quarter, Q4 = fourth quarter, US = United States, USD = United States dollar.

Notes:

1. Emerging East Asia is defined to include member states of the Association of Southeast Asian Nations plus the People's Republic of China; Hong Kong, China; and the Republic of Korea.
2. The EU-20 includes the member markets of Austria, Belgium, Croatia, Cyprus, Estonia, Finland, France, Germany, Greece, Ireland, Italy, Latvia, Lithuania, Luxembourg, Malta, the Netherlands, Portugal, Slovakia, Slovenia, and Spain.

Source: *AsianBondsOnline* calculations based on various local market sources.

[11] Emerging East Asia is defined to include member states of the Association of Southeast Asian Nations plus the People's Republic of China; Hong Kong, China; and the Republic of Korea.

Bond market expansions in the PRC and the Republic of Korea drove overall growth in the region's LCY bond market in Q2 2025 (Figure 2A). The PRC's bond market (USD23.1 trillion) expanded 3.5% q-o-q on robust growth in both the government and corporate bond segments. The Republic of Korea's LCY bonds outstanding tallied USD2.5 trillion at the end of June; its market led the region in terms of LCY bond market size as a share of gross domestic product (130.0%) (**Figure 2B**). Together, these two markets accounted for nearly 90% of the region's total LCY bond stock at the end of June (**Figure 2C**). Outstanding LCY bonds among members of the Association of Southeast Asian Nations (ASEAN) rose 1.0% q-o-q to USD2.6 trillion at the end of June and comprised 9.1% of the regional total.

Outstanding Treasury bonds in emerging East Asia are predominantly medium- and long-term securities. Treasury and other government bonds outstanding reached USD18.5 trillion at the end of June, representing 64.6% of the region's LCY bond market. Corporate bonds (USD9.4 trillion) and central bank bonds (USD0.7 trillion) comprised the remaining 33.0% and 2.3% shares, respectively. At the end of June, about 55% of outstanding Treasuries had a remaining tenor of more than 5 years (**Figure 2D**). As a result, the size-weighted average tenor of outstanding Treasury bonds in the region was 8.8 years at the end of June, compared with 7.9 years in the United States and 8.3 years in the European Union 20. In ASEAN markets, the size-weighted average tenor of outstanding Treasuries was longer at 9.0 years, owing to the predominance of long-dated government bonds in these markets, particularly in Thailand, Viet Nam, Singapore, and Malaysia.

Figure 2: Local Currency Bonds Outstanding in Select Emerging East Asian Markets

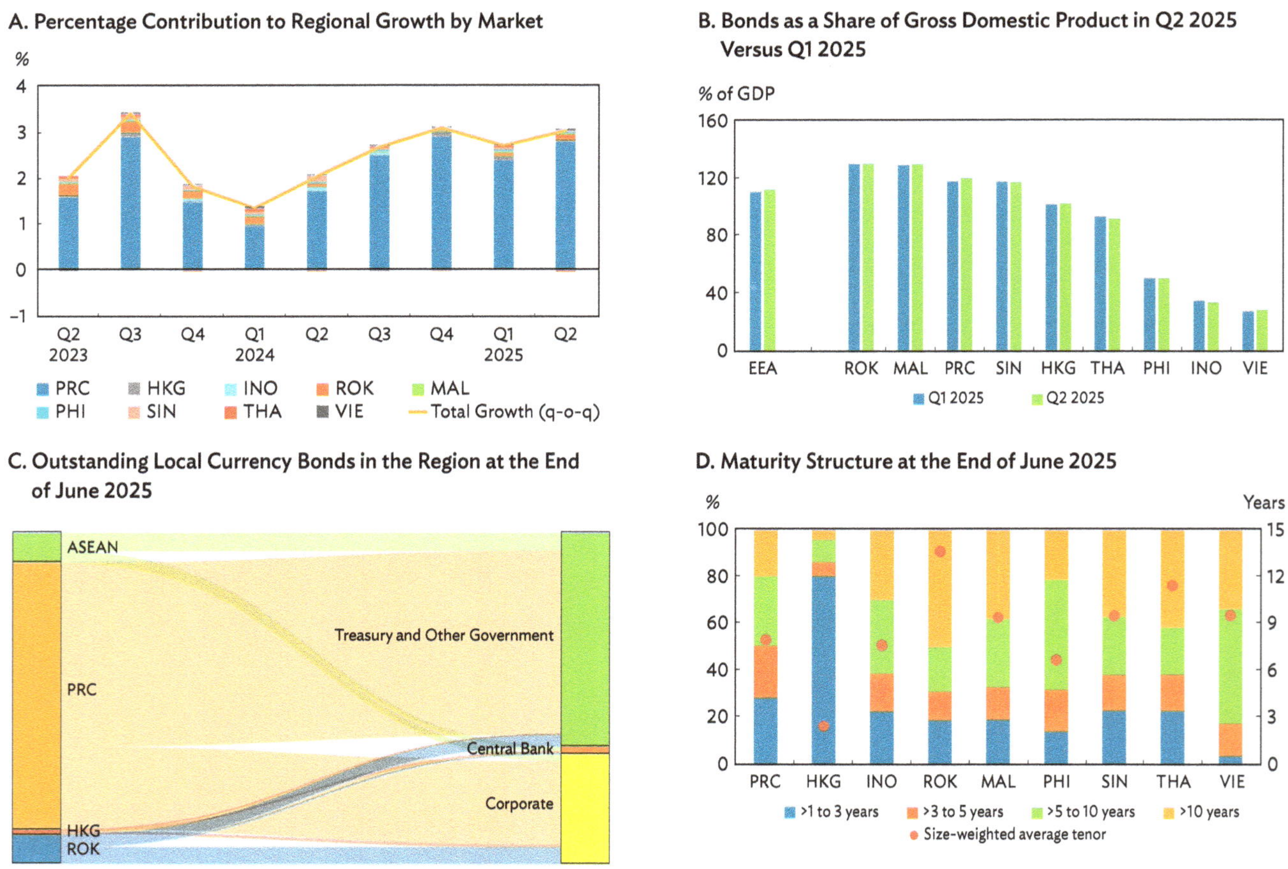

ASEAN = Association of Southeast Asian Nations; PRC = People's Republic of China; EEA = emerging East Asia; GDP = gross domestic product; HKG = Hong Kong, China; INO = Indonesia; ROK = Republic of Korea; MAL = Malaysia; PHI = Philippines; Q1 = first quarter; Q2 = second quarter; Q3 = third quarter; Q4 = fourth quarter; q-o-q = quarter-on-quarter; SIN = Singapore; THA = Thailand; VIE = Viet Nam.

Notes:

1. Emerging East Asia is defined to include member states of the Association of Southeast Asian Nations plus the People's Republic of China; Hong Kong, China; and the Republic of Korea.
2. Growth rates are calculated from a local currency base and do not include currency effects. For emerging East Asia, growth figures are based on 30 June 2025 currency exchange rates and do not include currency effects.
3. GDP data are from CEIC Company.

Source: *AsianBondsOnline* calculations based on various local market sources.

Investor diversity continued to improve in Treasury bond markets in emerging East Asia. Banks and insurance and pension funds remained the two largest investor groups in the region's Treasury bond market in Q2 2025, with average regional holding shares of 34.6% and 29.4%, respectively, at the end of June, compared to 35.9% and 29.0% a year earlier (**Figure 3**). Nearly all markets in the region recorded annual declines in bank holdings of Treasury bonds, while all other investor groups posted an increase in their respective holding shares at the end of June. The region's average holding shares for insurance and pension funds witnessed a minor increase to 29.4% in June from 29.0% in the prior year. Central bank holdings rose to 5.7% from 5.4% during the same period, buoyed by a substantial increase in Indonesia and smaller gains in Malaysia and Thailand. The central bank is the largest investor in the Treasury bond market of Indonesia: Bank Indonesia continues to engage in bond purchases in both the primary and secondary markets to support its monetary operations. Amid expectations of continued central bank easing in the region, the foreign holdings share rose to 10.8% in June from 10.6% a year earlier. While the investor profile for the region has remained stable overall, there have been small, continued improvements in investor diversification among regional bond markets, as evidenced by declining Herfindahl–Hirschman Index scores across the region.[12]

Figure 3: Investor Profiles of Local Currency Treasury Bonds in Select Emerging East Asian Markets

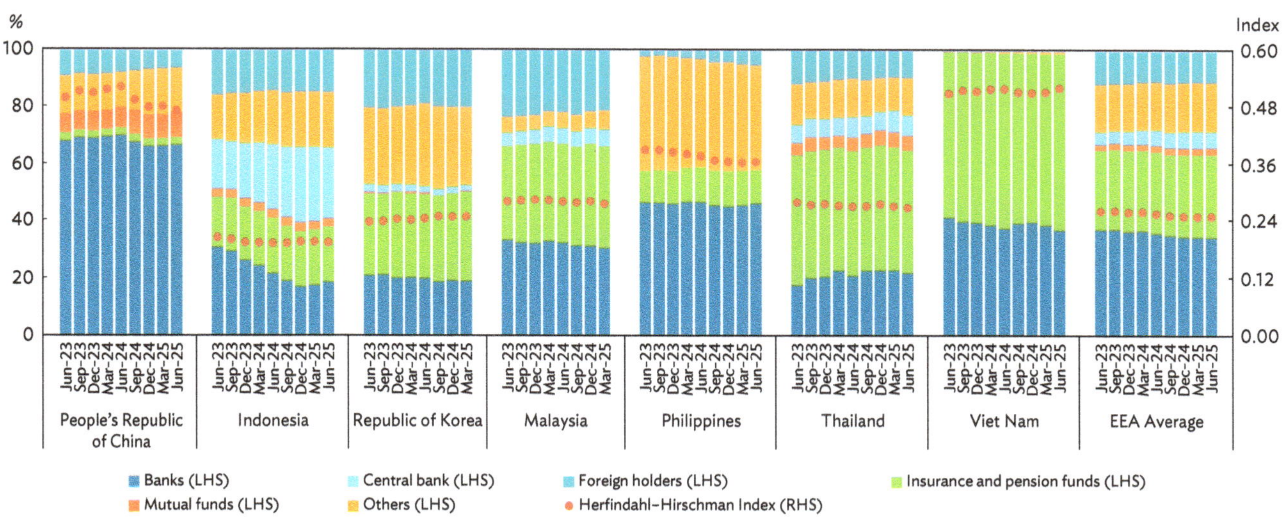

EEA = emerging East Asia, LHS = left-hand side, RHS = right-hand side.

Notes:

1. Data for the Republic of Korea and Malaysia are up to March 2025.
2. "Others" include government institutions, individuals, securities companies, custodians, private corporations, and all other investors not elsewhere classified.
3. The Herfindahl–Hirschman Index is a commonly accepted measure of market concentration. In this case, the index was used to measure the investor profile diversification of the local currency bond markets and is calculated by summing the squared share of each investor group in the bond market. A lower score indicates greater diversity.

Sources: People's Republic of China (CEIC Data Company); Indonesia (Directorate General of Budget Financing and Risk Management, Ministry of Finance); Republic of Korea (Bank of Korea); Malaysia (Bank Negara Malaysia); Philippines (Bureau of the Treasury); Thailand (Bank of Thailand); and Viet Nam (Ministry of Finance).

[12] The Herfindahl–Hirschman Index is a commonly accepted measure of market concentration. The index is used to measure the investor profile diversification of the region's local currency bond markets and is calculated by summing the squared share of each investor group in the bond market. A lower score indicates greater diversity.

Section 2. Local Currency Bond Issuance

LCY bond issuance in emerging East Asia rebounded in Q2 2025 amid continued monetary easing in most regional markets. Total LCY bond issuance rose to USD3.1 trillion in Q2 2025 on growth of 14.8% q-o-q, reversing a 0.6% q-o-q contraction in Q1 2025. The rebound in issuance was supported by increased bond sales from both the government and corporate bond segments (**Figure 4A**).

Government bond issuance in the region increased 18.3% q-o-q as most governments continued front-loading their funding needs during the quarter:

- Government bond issuance in the PRC expanded 19.7% q-o-q and comprised 87.2% of the regional total in Q2 2025 (**Figure 4B**). This growth was in line with the government's planned increase in annual bond issuance to boost the economy. In March, the Government of the PRC raised its quotas for the issuance of long-term special Treasury bonds and local government bonds, and announced the additional issuance of special Treasury bonds to recapitalize state-owned banks.
- Issuance in ASEAN markets rose 9.3% q-o-q in Q2 2025, largely driven by notable government bond issuances in Singapore and the Philippines. In Singapore, the government issued SGD3.0 billion worth of green bonds in April as part of its Green Bond Framework. Also in April, the Government of the Philippines raised an outsized PHP300.0 billion worth of new 10-year benchmark bonds.

Total corporate bond issuance in the region surged 25.2% q-o-q in Q2 2025 amid monetary easing in most regional markets. Growth largely stemmed from the PRC (28.9% q-o-q) and the Republic of Korea (16.0% q-o-q) as companies took advantage of lower interest rates following rate cuts in May by both the People's Bank of China and the Bank of Korea. Viet Nam registered a surge in issuance in Q2 2025, with its corporate bond issuance increasing more than tenfold as banks raised capital to meet the high credit growth target set by the central bank and nonfinancial firms sought to meet their refinancing needs.

Figure 4: Local Currency Bond Issuance in Select Emerging East Asian Markets

A. Percentage Contribution to Growth by Bond Type | **B. Market Structure in the Second Quarter of 2025**

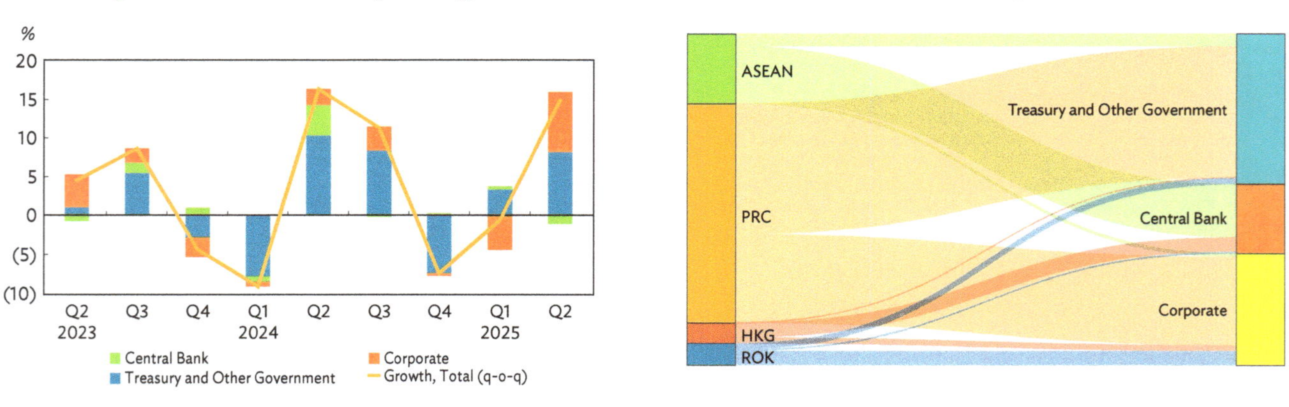

( ) = negative; ASEAN = Association of Southeast Asian Nations; PRC = People's Republic of China; HKG = Hong Kong, China; ROK = Republic of Korea; Q1 = first quarter; Q2 = second quarter; Q3 = third quarter; Q4 = fourth quarter; q-o-q = quarter-on-quarter.

Notes:
1. ASEAN comprises the markets of Indonesia, Malaysia, the Philippines, Singapore, Thailand, and Viet Nam.
2. Figures were computed based on 30 June 2025 currency exchange rates and do not include currency effects.

Source: *AsianBondsOnline* calculations based on various local market sources.

LCY government bond issuance in emerging East Asia continued to be dominated by medium- to long-term maturities in Q2 2025, extending the region's average issuance maturity compared with the previous quarter. The share of government bonds issued with maturities of more than 5 years rose to 60.4% in Q2 2025 from 52.8% in the previous quarter (**Figure 5A**). Consequently, the size-weighted average maturity of Treasury bond issuance increased to 9.9 years in Q2 2025 from 7.6 years in Q1 2025:

- The share of medium- to long-term bond issuances in the PRC rose to 58.8% from 47.3% during the review period, driven by the issuance of CNY555.0 billion of long-term special Treasury bonds (20–50 years) during the quarter. Further, the size-weighted average maturity of the PRC's bond issuance increased to 9.3 years from 6.5 years in Q1 2025 (**Figure 5B**).
- The medium- to long-term issuance share in the Republic of Korea increased to 78.5% from 68.1% during the review period, increasing the market's size-weighted average maturity to 15.6 years in Q2 2025, up from 14.5 years in Q1 2025. The increase was driven by the government's continued issuance of bonds with maturities of 20–50 years.
- ASEAN markets continued to have the largest shares of medium- to long-term maturities in the region, particularly the Philippines (94.7%), Malaysia (80.6%), and Viet Nam (78.2%). The size-weighted average maturity of government bonds issued in ASEAN markets remained above 10.0 years in Q2 2025, led by Thailand and Malaysia at 12.7 years and 12.1 years, respectively (**Figures 6A and 6B**). Thailand and Indonesia issued government bonds with the longest maturities in Q2 2025 at 47 years and 39 years, respectively, as part of their regular auction schedules and to meet the demand for long-duration bonds among insurance companies and pension funds.

Figure 5: Maturity Structure of Local Currency Treasury Bond Issuance in Select Emerging East Asian Markets

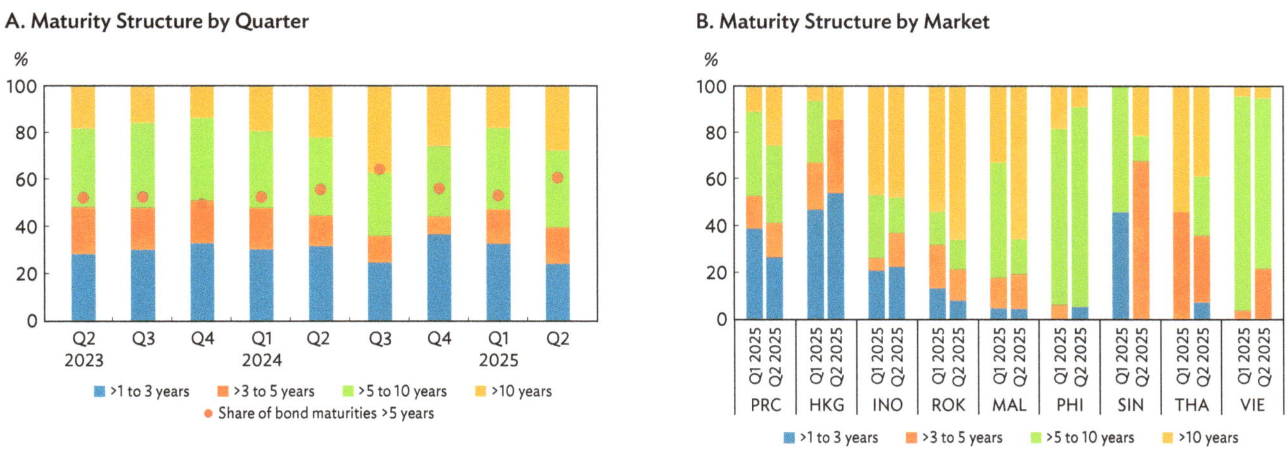

PRC = People's Republic of China; HKG = Hong Kong, China; INO = Indonesia; ROK = Republic of Korea; MAL = Malaysia; PHI = Philippines; Q1 = first quarter; Q2 = second quarter; Q3 = third quarter; Q4 = fourth quarter; SIN = Singapore; THA = Thailand; VIE = Viet Nam.

Notes:

1. Figures were computed based on 30 June 2025 currency exchange rates and do not include currency effects.
2. Treasury bonds are local-currency-denominated, fixed-income securities issued by a government with maturities longer than 1 year.

Source: *AsianBondsOnline* calculations based on various local market sources.

Figure 6: Average Size-Weighted Maturity of Treasury Bond Issuance in Select Emerging East Asian Markets

A. Average Size-Weighted Maturity by Subgroup

B. Average Size-Weighted Maturity by Market

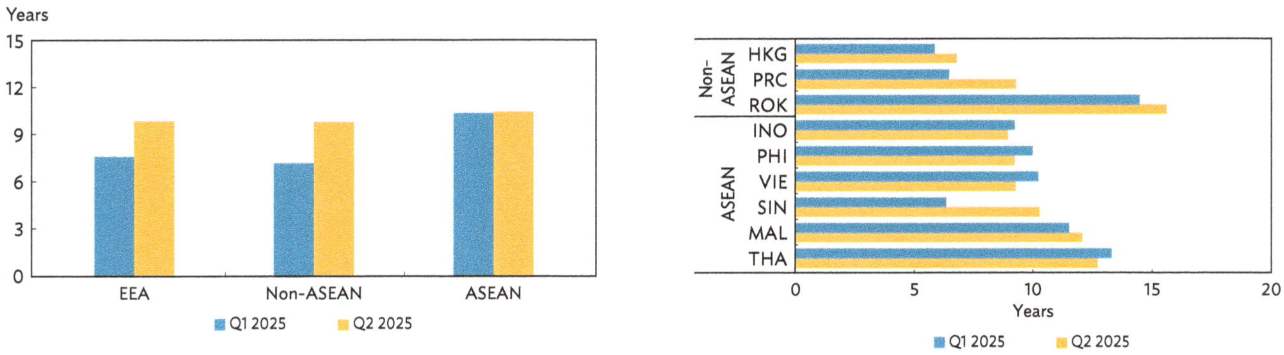

ASEAN = Association of Southeast Asian Nations; PRC = People's Republic of China; EEA = emerging East Asia; HKG = Hong Kong, China; INO = Indonesia; ROK = Republic of Korea; MAL = Malaysia; PHI = Philippines; Q1 = first quarter; Q2 = second quarter; SIN = Singapore; THA = Thailand; VIE = Viet Nam.

Notes:
1. Figures were computed based on 30 June 2025 currency exchange rates and do not include currency effects.
2. Treasury bonds are local-currency-denominated, fixed-income securities issued by a government with maturities longer than 1 year.

Source: *AsianBondsOnline* calculations based on various local market sources.

Section 3: Intra-Regional Bond Issuance

Emerging East Asia's intra-regional bond issuance recovered in Q2 2025 amid a favorable interest rate environment in the region.[13] The region's intra-regional bond issuance grew 62.0% q-o-q in Q2 2025, tallying USD12.6 billion and reversing the 31.1% q-o-q contraction in Q1 2025 (**Figure 7A**):

- Increased debt sales from Hong Kong, China; the PRC; Singapore; and Malaysia were the main contributors to quarterly growth. Hong Kong, China, whose total intra-regional bond issuance grew 51.7% q-o-q to USD9.6 billion in Q2 2025, remained the region's top issuer, accounting for 75.8% of the total. This was followed by the PRC, whose total issuance surged more than 16 times to USD1.5 billion from USD0.1 billion in the previous quarter, representing 11.9% of the region's total quarterly issuance. The Republic of Korea posted a 52.1% q-o-q decline in issuance in Q2 2025, which fell to USD0.4 billion, as corporate issuers scaled back their issuance sizes compared with the previous quarter.
- The finance sector dominated the region's intra-regional bond issuance during the quarter, representing 46.5% of the total (**Figure 7B**). Across corporate issuers, China Merchants Group—a logistics company headquartered in Hong Kong, China—maintained its position as the region's leading corporate issuer (CNY13.5 billion), representing 14.9% of the regional total with its combined issuances. This was followed by Ping An Insurance Group (HKD11.8 billion), a financial firm and the sole issuer from the PRC during the quarter with a single issuance that accounted for 11.9% of the region's total.
- The Chinese yuan was the preferred currency of intra-regional issuance, accounting for a 74.3% share. There were two CNY-denominated sustainable bond issuances from Hong Kong, China during the quarter: green bonds worth CNY4.0 billion and CNY1.0 billion issued by the Government of the Hong Kong Special Administrative Region of the People's Republic of China and China Everbright Greentech, respectively.

[13] Intra-regional bond issuance is defined as emerging East Asian bond issuance denominated in a regional currency excluding the issuer's home currency.

- While short- to medium-term financing continued to dominate intra-regional bond issuance in emerging East Asia in Q2 2025, the average maturity still increased. Issuances with a maturity of 5 years or less accounted for a 75.0% share in Q2 2025, down from the previous quarter's 80.1% (**Figure 7C**). This trend was driven by an increase in the share of bonds with maturities of more than 10 years, which climbed to 15.9% in Q2 2025 from 8.3% in the previous quarter, steered by Hong Kong, China's CNY-denominated green and infrastructure bonds with 20-year and 30-year maturities, respectively, as well as Nomura International Fund's KRW-denominated bond with a maturity of 15 years. Additionally, the share of bond issuances with maturities of over 3 years and up to 5 years rose to 25.7% from 12.6% during the same period. Overall, the size-weighted average maturity of intra-regional bond issuance reached 5.5 years, up from 2.8 years in the previous quarter (**Figure 7D**).

Figure 7: Intra-Regional Bond Issuance in Select Emerging East Asian Markets

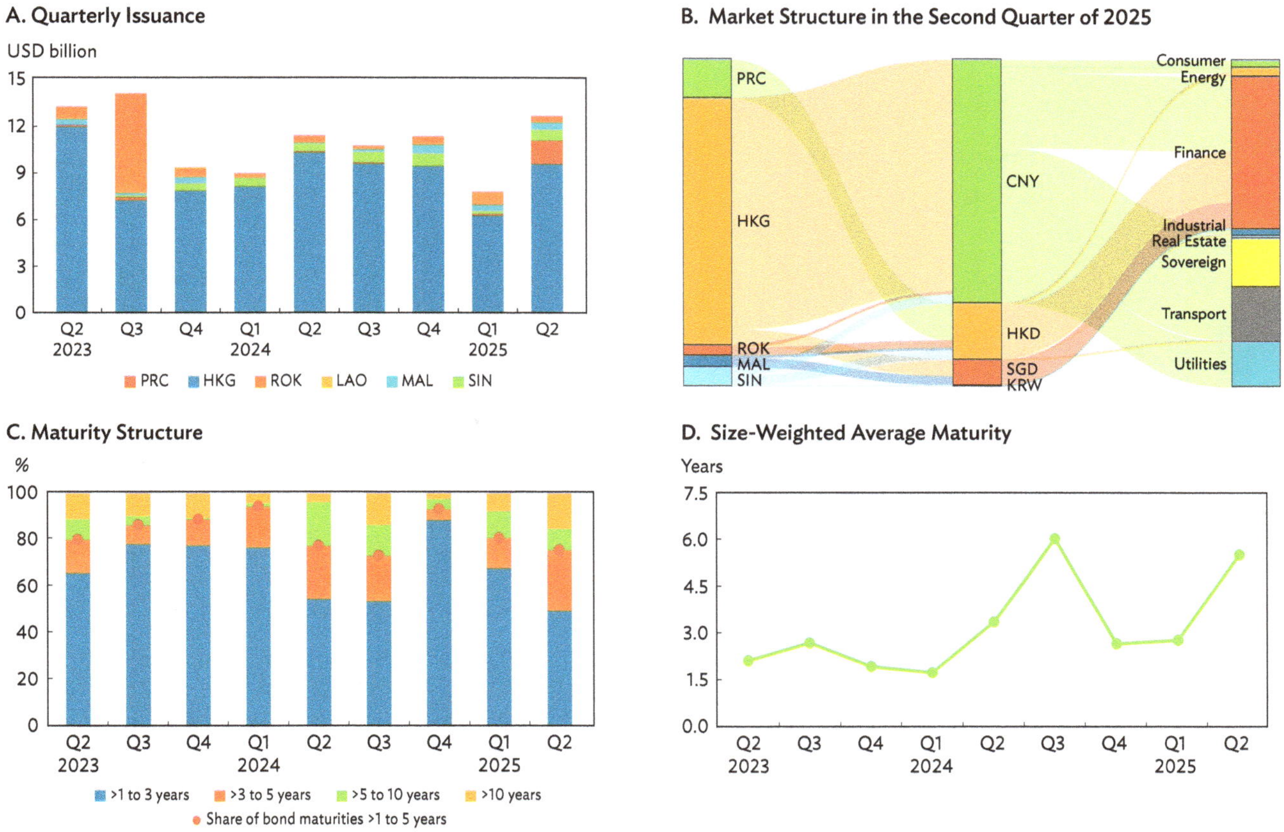

PRC = People's Republic of China; CNY = Chinese yuan; HKD = Hong Kong dollar; HKG = Hong Kong, China; ROK = Republic of Korea; KRW = Korean won; LAO = Lao People's Democratic Republic; MAL = Malaysia; Q1 = first quarter; Q2 = second quarter; Q3 = third quarter; Q4 = fourth quarter; SGD = Singapore dollar; SIN = Singapore; USD = United States dollar.

Notes:

1. Emerging East Asia is defined to include member states of the Association of Southeast Asian Nations plus the People's Republic of China; Hong Kong, China; and the Republic of Korea.
2. Intra-regional bond issuance is defined as emerging East Asian bond issuance denominated in a regional currency excluding the issuer's home currency.
3. Figures were computed based on 30 June 2025 currency exchange rates and do not include currency effects.

Source: *AsianBondsOnline* calculations based on Bloomberg LP data.

Section 4. G3 Currency Bond Issuance

Emerging East Asian G3 currency bond issuance rose in Q2 2025, largely driven by corporate bond issuance to finance capital investments.[14] G3 currency bond issuance in the region reached USD74.1 billion in Q2 2025 on growth of 1.1% q-o-q, slowing from the previous quarter's 17.7% q-o-q growth (**Figure 8A**). Issuance from ASEAN economies tallied USD22.7 billion, accounting for 30.6% of regional G3 bond issuance in Q2 2025 and reflecting growth of 4.6% q-o-q, buoyed by increased issuance in Malaysia and Singapore (**Figure 8B**):

- Among all regional markets, the top issuer of G3 currency bonds in Q2 2025 was MTR Corporation, which issued USD6.1 billion worth of USD-denominated securities to support infrastructure projects and enhance its capital structure.
- Several regional economies recorded notable q-o-q increases in issuance, including Malaysia (145.9%) and Singapore (73.0%), as well as Hong Kong, China (50.3%), where G3 issuance was primarily driven by corporates.

Figure 8: G3 Currency Bond Issuance in Select Emerging East Asian Markets

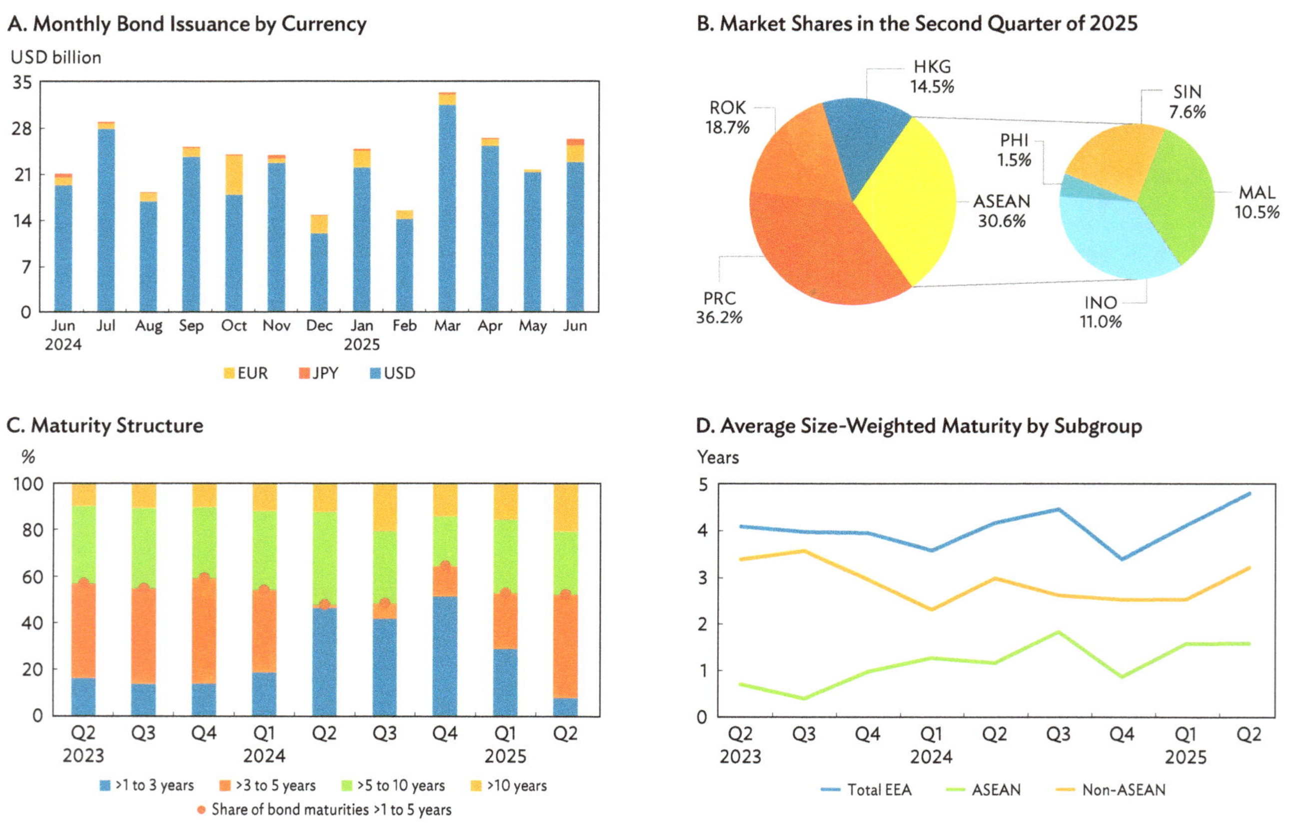

ASEAN = Association of Southeast Asian Nations; PRC = People's Republic of China; EEA = emerging East Asia; EUR = euro; HKG = Hong Kong, China; INO = Indonesia; JPY = Japanese yen; ROK = Republic of Korea; MAL = Malaysia; PHI = Philippines; Q1 = first quarter; Q2 = second quarter; Q3 = third quarter; Q4 = fourth quarter; SIN = Singapore; USD = United States dollar.

Notes:

1. Emerging East Asia is defined to include the member states of ASEAN plus the People's Republic of China; Hong Kong, China; and the Republic of Korea. ASEAN comprises the markets of Indonesia, Malaysia, the Philippines, Singapore, Thailand, and Viet Nam.
2. G3 currency bonds are denominated in either euros, Japanese yen, or United States dollars.
3. Figures were computed based on 30 June 2025 currency exchange rates and do not include currency effects.

Source: *AsianBondsOnline* calculations based on Bloomberg LP data.

[14] G3 currency bonds are bonds denominated in either euros, Japanese yen, or United States dollars.

Hong Kong, China's MTR Corporation issued a total of USD6.1 billion worth of G3 currency bonds during the quarter to fund infrastructure operations and strengthen its capital structure, while Malaysia's Petronas issued USD5.0 billion worth of USD-denominated bonds to support its corporate expenditures.
- The PRC recorded the most G3 issuance among all regional markets at USD26.9 billion, although this represented a 13.7% q-o-q contraction as investor appetite waned over heightened default concerns (page 39, para. 3).

Short-term maturities of 5 years or less made up about half (52.2%) of G3 bond issuance in Q2 2025, with tenors of over 3 to 5 years accounting for 44.6% of total G3 bond issuance, up from the previous quarter's 23.9% (**Figure 8C**). This resulted in the size-weighted average maturity of regional G3 bond issuance ticking up to 4.8 years in Q2 2025 from 4.1 years in Q1 2025 (**Figure 8D**).

Appendix

Table A1: Size and Composition of Select Emerging East Asian Local Currency Bond Markets

	Q2 2024		Q1 2025		Q2 2025			Growth Rate (%) Q2 2025	
	Amount (USD billion)	% of GDP	Amount (USD billion)	% of GDP	Amount (USD billion)	% share	% of GDP	q-o-q	y-o-y
People's Republic of China									
Total	19,971	110.0	22,012	117.2	23,072	100.0	120.1	3.5	13.9
Treasury and Other Government	13,320	73.4	15,090	80.3	15,882	68.8	82.7	3.9	17.5
Central Bank	2	0.01	0	0.0	0	0.0	0.0	–	(100.0)
Corporate	6,649	36.6	6,922	36.9	7,190	31.2	37.4	2.5	6.6
Hong Kong, China									
Total	389	98.4	417	101.2	422	100.0	102.3	2.0	9.1
Treasury and Other Government	33	8.4	40	9.6	37	8.9	9.1	(4.9)	13.6
Central Bank	164	41.5	169	41.1	169	40.0	41.0	0.5	3.4
Corporate	191	48.4	208	50.5	215	51.1	52.2	4.4	13.2
Indonesia									
Total	440	33.6	473	34.8	482	100.0	34.2	(0.1)	8.8
Treasury and Other Government	364	27.9	387	28.4	399	82.8	28.3	1.3	8.7
Central Bank	47	3.6	58	4.2	52	10.8	3.7	(11.3)	10.3
Corporate	28	2.2	29	2.1	31	6.4	2.2	3.4	7.4
Republic of Korea									
Total	2,392	132.1	2,257	129.3	2,490	100.0	130.0	1.4	2.4
Treasury and Other Government	911	50.3	869	49.8	978	39.3	51.1	3.5	5.6
Central Bank	87	4.8	75	4.3	78	3.1	4.1	(4.7)	(11.5)
Corporate	1,394	77.0	1,313	75.2	1,433	57.6	74.8	0.3	1.1
Malaysia									
Total	437	128.1	482	128.4	518	100.0	129.5	1.9	6.0
Treasury and Other Government	254	74.5	282	74.9	304	58.7	76.0	2.6	6.9
Central Bank	0.4	0.1	0	0.0	0	0.0	0.0	–	(100.0)
Corporate	182	53.4	201	53.4	214	41.3	53.5	1.1	4.8
Philippines									
Total	214	49.3	235	50.0	245	100.0	50.5	2.7	10.3
Treasury and Other Government	178	41.0	196	41.8	210	85.5	43.2	5.2	13.3
Central Bank	14	3.2	16	3.4	13	5.3	2.7	(18.9)	(10.4)
Corporate	22	5.0	23	4.9	22	9.2	4.6	(4.0)	(1.3)
Singapore									
Total	606	116.6	646	117.1	686	100.0	117.3	0.6	6.1
Treasury and Other Government	222	42.7	237	43.0	252	36.7	43.1	0.7	6.4
Central Bank	238	45.7	257	46.7	277	40.4	47.4	1.9	9.3
Corporate	146	28.1	151	27.4	157	22.9	26.8	(1.8)	0.7
Thailand									
Total	460	92.7	512	92.8	529	100.0	91.6	(1.0)	1.8
Treasury and Other Government	269	54.2	306	55.4	321	60.6	55.5	0.4	5.4
Central Bank	61	12.2	73	13.2	72	13.6	12.5	(5.3)	4.9
Corporate	130	26.2	133	24.2	137	25.8	23.6	(2.0)	(7.2)
Viet Nam									
Total	115	26.9	126	27.4	134	100.0	28.8	8.2	19.3
Treasury and Other Government	81	19.0	91	19.7	92	68.8	19.8	3.5	16.3
Central Bank	6	1.4	4	0.8	6	4.8	1.4	77.2	11.1
Corporate	28	6.5	32	6.9	35	26.4	7.6	13.6	29.8
Emerging East Asia									
Total	25,022	104.8	27,161	109.9	28,578	100.0	112.2	3.0	12.0
Treasury and Other Government	15,632	65.4	17,497	70.8	18,475	64.6	72.6	3.7	16.0
Central Bank	619	2.6	652	2.6	668	2.3	2.6	(1.3)	3.7
Corporate	8,771	36.7	9,012	36.5	9,435	33.0	37.1	2.1	5.5
Japan									
Total	8,559	230.5	9,326	227.1	9,763	100.0	225.7	0.6	2.1
Treasury and Other Government	7,889	212.5	8,593	209.2	8,990	92.1	207.8	0.5	2.0
Central Bank	23	0.6	21	0.5	21	0.2	0.5	(2.7)	(17.4)
Corporate	647	17.4	712	17.3	753	7.7	17.4	1.6	4.2

( ) = negative, – = not applicable, GDP = gross domestic product, Q1 = first quarter, Q2 = second quarter, q-o-q = quarter-on-quarter, USD = United States dollar, y-o-y = year-on-year.

Notes:

1. Emerging East Asia is defined to include the member states of ASEAN plus the People's Republic of China; Hong Kong, China; and the Republic of Korea.
2. For Singapore, corporate bonds outstanding are based on *AsianBondsOnline* estimates.
3. Growth rates are calculated from a local currency base and do not include currency effects. For emerging East Asia, growth figures are based on 30 June 2025 currency exchange rates and do not include currency effects.
4. GDP data are from CEIC Data Company.
5. Bloomberg LP end-of-period local currency–USD rates are used.

Sources: People's Republic of China (CEIC Data Company); Hong Kong, China (Hong Kong Monetary Authority); Indonesia (Bank Indonesia; Directorate General of Budget Financing and Risk Management, Ministry of Finance; and Indonesia Stock Exchange); Japan (Japan Securities Dealers Association); Republic of Korea (Bank of Korea and KG Zeroin Corporation); Malaysia (Bank Negara Malaysia); Philippines (Bangko Sentral ng Pilipinas, Bureau of the Treasury, and Bloomberg LP); Singapore (Monetary Authority of Singapore and Bloomberg LP); Thailand (Bank of Thailand); and Viet Nam (Hanoi Stock Exchange, State Bank of Vietnam, Vietnam Bond Market Association, and Bloomberg LP).

Table A2: Local-Currency-Denominated Bond Issuance

	Q2 2024		Q1 2025		Q2 2025		Growth Rate (%)	
	Amount (USD billion)	% share	Amount (USD billion)	% share	Amount (USD billion)	% share	Q2 2025	
							q-o-q	y-o-y
People's Republic of China								
Total	1,609	100.0	1,652	100.0	2,062	100.0	23.2	26.3
Treasury and Other Government	923	57.4	1,019	61.7	1,235	59.9	19.7	31.9
Central Bank	0	0.0	0	0.0	0	0.0	–	–
Corporate	686	42.6	633	38.3	827	40.1	28.9	18.9
Hong Kong, China								
Total	163	100.0	180	100.0	184	100.0	3.2	13.4
Treasury and Other Government	0.2	0.1	1	0.5	2	0.9	80.0	800.0
Central Bank	130	79.8	135	74.8	135	73.2	1.0	4.1
Corporate	33	20.1	44	25	48	25.8	8.1	45.7
Indonesia								
Total	46	100.0	39	100.0	39	100.0	(0.7)	(16.6)
Treasury and Other Government	12	25.7	16	40.7	16	40.9	(0.1)	32.8
Central Bank	32	69.8	20	52.2	21	53.4	1.5	(36.3)
Corporate	2	4.5	3	7.1	2	5.8	(19.9)	5.6
Republic of Korea								
Total	176	100.0	169	100.0	205	100.0	11.3	14.7
Treasury and Other Government	49	27.8	50	29.6	60	29.3	10.2	20.9
Central Bank	16	9.1	15	8.8	13	6.5	(18.0)	(18.2)
Corporate	111	63.1	104	61.6	132	64.2	16.0	16.7
Malaysia								
Total	25	100.0	22	100.0	21	100.0	(12.9)	(25.4)
Treasury and Other Government	13	53.7	12	51.7	10	46.1	(22.3)	(36.0)
Central Bank	3	10.3	0	0.0	0	0.0	–	(100.0)
Corporate	9	36.0	11	48.3	11	53.9	(2.7)	11.8
Philippines								
Total	45	100.0	47	100.0	48	100.0	0.5	2.5
Treasury and Other Government	10	22.9	15	30.9	20	40.6	32.0	82.1
Central Bank	34	75.5	31	66.3	28	57.3	(13.2)	(22.2)
Corporate	1	1.6	1	2.7	1	2.1	(23.5)	30.0
Singapore								
Total	417	100.0	421	100.0	451	100.0	1.4	1.3
Treasury and Other Government	46	11.1	41	9.7	52	11.5	19.9	4.9
Central Bank	368	88.1	377	89.5	398	88.3	0.1	1.5
Corporate	3	0.8	3	0.8	1	0.2	(70.6)	(70.8)
Thailand								
Total	62	100.0	63	100.0	67	100.0	2.2	(4.0)
Treasury and Other Government	18	29.9	18	28.4	19	28.3	2.0	(9.1)
Central Bank	30	48.1	35	55.8	38	56.0	2.7	11.8
Corporate	14	22.0	10	15.9	10	15.7	0.8	(31.5)
Viet Nam								
Total	29	100.0	49	100.0	28	100.0	(40.2)	1.0
Treasury and Other Government	3	10.4	4	8.9	3	12.2	(17.6)	19.2
Central Bank	23	79.4	44	89.8	19	65.2	(56.6)	(17.2)
Corporate	3	10.2	0.6	1.3	6	22.6	932.4	123.6
Emerging East Asia								
Total	2,572	100.0	2,642	100.0	3,105	100.0	14.8	17.7
Treasury and Other Government	1,075	41.8	1,175	44.5	1,416	45.6	18.3	29.1
Central Bank	636	24.7	656	24.8	651	21.0	(4.2)	(2.1)
Corporate	861	33.5	811	30.7	1,038	33.4	25.2	18.6
Japan								
Total	330	100.0	346	100.0	370	100.0	2.8	0.4
Treasury and Other Government	296	89.8	329	94.9	333	90.0	(2.6)	0.6
Central Bank	0	0.0	0	0.0	0	0.0	–	–
Corporate	34	10.2	18	5.1	37	10.0	101.6	(1.8)

( ) = negative, – = not applicable, Q1 = first quarter, Q2 = second quarter, q-o-q = quarter-on-quarter, USD = United States dollar, y-o-y = year-on-year.

Notes:

1. Data reflect gross bond issuance.
2. Bloomberg LP end-of-period local currency–USD rates are used.
3. Growth rates are calculated from a local currency base and do not include currency effects. For emerging East Asia, growth figures are based on 30 June 2025 currency exchange rates and do not include currency effects.

Sources: People's Republic of China (CEIC Data Company); Hong Kong, China (Hong Kong Monetary Authority); Indonesia (Bank Indonesia, Directorate General of Budget Financing and Risk Management, Ministry of Finance; and Indonesia Stock Exchange); Japan (Japan Securities Dealers Association); Republic of Korea (Bank of Korea and KG Zeroin Corporation); Malaysia (Bank Negara Malaysia); Philippines (Bangko Sentral ng Pilipinas, Bureau of the Treasury, and Bloomberg LP); Singapore (Monetary Authority of Singapore and Bloomberg LP); Thailand (Bank of Thailand and Thai Bond Market Association); and Viet Nam (Hanoi Stock Exchange, State Bank of Vietnam, Vietnam Bond Market Association, and Bloomberg LP).

Recent Developments in the ASEAN+3 Sustainable Bond Market

Sustainable Bonds Outstanding

Expansion of the ASEAN+3 sustainable bond market accelerated in the second quarter (Q2) of 2025, supported by robust issuance on improved financial conditions.[15] Sustainable bonds outstanding in ASEAN+3 reached USD955.3 billion at the end of June, expanding 3.3% quarter-on-quarter (q-o-q) in Q2 2025, up from tepid 0.5% q-o-q growth in the prior quarter. The pace of expansion during the quarter also exceeded that of the sustainable bond market globally (2.6% q-o-q) and in the European Union 20 (EU-20) (3.1% q-o-q). ASEAN+3 remained the second-largest regional sustainable bond market in the world, accounting for 18.3% of the global total of USD5.2 trillion at the end of Q2 2025 (**Figure 9**). However, ASEAN+3's sustainable bond market comprised only 2.4% of its general bond market, compared with the corresponding 8.5% share in the EU-20. The People's Republic of China (PRC) (USD385.6 billion) accounted for 40.4% of total ASEAN+3 sustainable bonds outstanding at the end of June, which was less than its equivalent share of 57.4% in the ASEAN+3 general bond market. ASEAN sustainable bonds outstanding accounted for 10.5% of the region's total sustainable bond stock, exceeding its corresponding share of 5.9% in ASEAN+3's general bond market. Larger contributions to the region's sustainable bond market versus its general bond market were also observed in the Republic of Korea (19.4% versus 5.5%) and Hong Kong, China (4.8% versus 0.6%).

ASEAN+3's sustainable bond market showed greater diversity in terms of instrument profile than the EU-20's. Green bonds accounted for 57.9% of total sustainable bonds outstanding in ASEAN+3 at the end of June (**Figure 10**), which was less than the corresponding share of 66.0% in the EU-20, reflecting a more diversified bond instrument profile. In ASEAN+3, the respective

Figure 9: Global Sustainable Bonds Outstanding

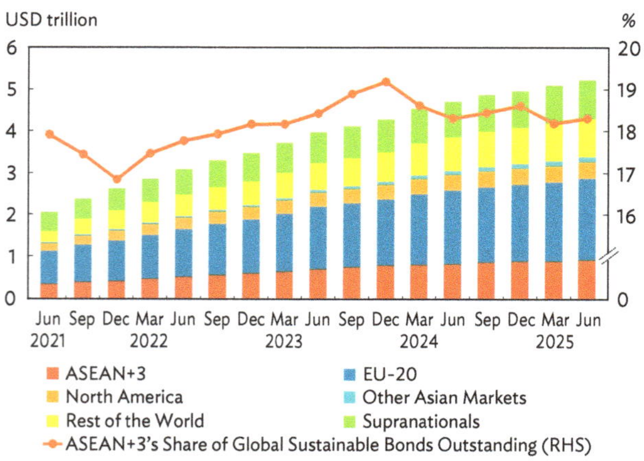

ASEAN+3 = Association of Southeast Asian Nations plus the People's Republic of China; Hong Kong, China; Japan; and the Republic of Korea; EU-20 = European Union 20; RHS = right-hand side; USD = United States dollar.

Notes:

1. The EU-20 includes EU member markets Austria, Belgium, Croatia, Cyprus, Estonia, Finland, France, Germany, Greece, Ireland, Italy, Latvia, Lithuania, Luxembourg, Malta, the Netherlands, Portugal, Slovakia, Slovenia, and Spain.
2. Data include both local currency and foreign currency issues.

Source: *AsianBondsOnline* calculations based on Bloomberg LP data.

Figure 10: Market Profile of Outstanding ASEAN+3 Sustainable Bonds at the End of June 2025

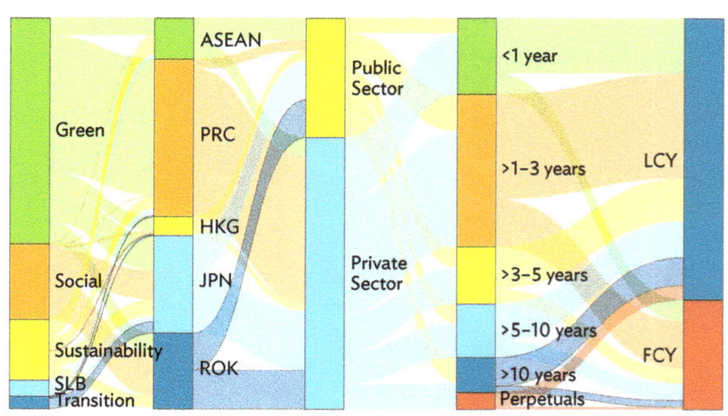

ASEAN = Association of Southeast Asian Nations; PRC = People's Republic of China; FCY = foreign currency; HKG = Hong Kong, China; JPN = Japan; ROK = Republic of Korea; LCY = local currency; SLB = sustainability-linked bond.

Notes:

1. ASEAN+3 is defined to include member states of ASEAN plus the People's Republic of China; Hong Kong, China; Japan; and the Republic of Korea.
2. ASEAN comprises the markets of Cambodia, Indonesia, the Lao People's Democratic Republic, Malaysia, the Philippines, Singapore, Thailand, and Viet Nam.
3. SLBs include transition-linked bonds.

Source: *AsianBondsOnline* calculations based on Bloomberg LP data.

[15] ASEAN+3 comprises the member states of the Association of Southeast Asian Nations (ASEAN) plus the People's Republic of China; Hong Kong, China; Japan; and the Republic of Korea.

shares of social bonds (19.5%), sustainability bonds (15.4%), and transition bonds (3.2%) exceeded their respective corresponding shares in the EU-20: 17.0%, 9.0%, and 0.3%, respectively (**Table 1**). This resulted in a lower Herfindahl–Hirschman Index score for ASEAN+3 of 0.40 versus 0.48 for the EU-20.[16] The private sector's share (69.5%) in sustainable bonds outstanding in ASEAN+3 was also higher than the corresponding share in the EU-20 (50.5%). The private sector accounted for a majority share of sustainable bonds outstanding in large regional markets such as the PRC (93.2%), Japan (60.0%), and the Republic of Korea (51.4%) (Figure 10). Public sector issuances comprised a majority of sustainable bonds outstanding in the markets of Hong Kong, China (57.6%) and ASEAN (53.2%). The local currency (LCY) financing shares of the EU-20 were comparable in its sustainable (90.1%) and general (89.5%) bond markets at the end of Q2 2025. This contrasts with ASEAN+3, where the LCY financing share in the sustainable bond market (72.1%) lagged that in the general bond market (95.5%).

Short- to medium-term financing dominated ASEAN+3's sustainable bond market at the end of June. Around 73.2% of outstanding sustainable bonds in ASEAN+3 had a remaining tenor of 5 years or less, which was well above the corresponding share of 48.0% in the EU-20 (**Figure 11**). Meanwhile, ASEAN markets had 64.0% of sustainable bonds outstanding with remaining tenors of over 5 years, driven by large, long-term sustainable bonds from governments in Indonesia, the Philippines, Singapore, and Thailand. ASEAN's size-weighted average tenor stood at 11.1 years at the end of June, exceeding that of both ASEAN+3 (4.6 years) and the EU-20 (7.7 years), with the longest average tenors seen in Singapore (16.6 years) and the Philippines (11.8 years). Social bonds had the shortest maturity structure in the ASEAN+3 sustainable bond

Table 1: Instrument, Issuer, and Currency Profiles in the ASEAN+3 and European Union 20 Sustainable Bond Markets at the End of June 2025

By End-June 2025	ASEAN+3	EU-20
Instrument profile (value-based share of regional sustainable bonds outstanding)		
Green bonds	57.9%	66.0%
Social bonds	19.5%	17.0%
Sustainability bonds	15.4%	9.0%
SLBs (including transition-linked bonds)	4.1%	7.7%
Transition bonds	3.2%	0.3%
Herfindahl–Hirschman Index	0.40	0.48
Issuer and currency profile		
Private sector's share of regional general bonds outstanding	23.9%	39.7%
Private sector's share of regional sustainable bonds outstanding	69.5%	50.5%
LCY financing's share of regional general bonds outstanding	95.5%	89.5%
LCY financing's share of regional sustainable bonds outstanding	72.1%	90.1%

ASEAN+3 = Association of Southeast Asian Nations plus the People's Republic of China; Hong Kong, China; Japan; and the Republic of Korea; EU-20 = European Union 20; LCY = local currency; SLB = sustainability-linked bond.

Note: The EU-20 includes European Union member markets Austria, Belgium, Croatia, Cyprus, Estonia, Finland, France, Germany, Greece, Ireland, Italy, Latvia, Lithuania, Luxembourg, Malta, the Netherlands, Portugal, Slovakia, Slovenia, and Spain.

Source: *AsianBondsOnline* calculations based on Bloomberg LP data.

Figure 11: Tenor Profiles of ASEAN+3 and European Union 20 Sustainable Bonds Outstanding at the End of June 2025

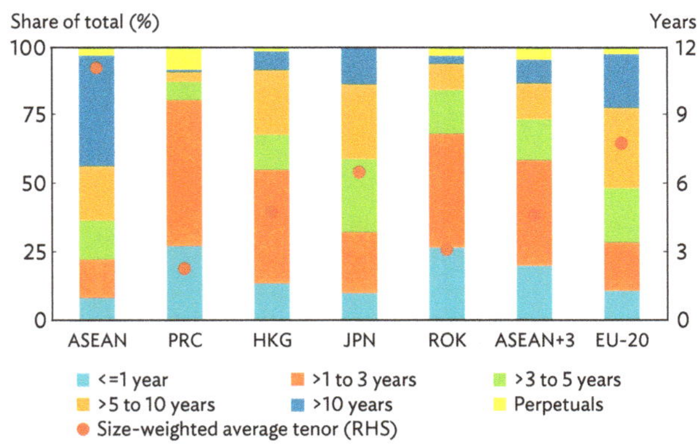

ASEAN = Association of Southeast Asian Nations; PRC = People's Republic of China; EU-20 = European Union 20; HKG = Hong Kong, China; JPN = Japan; ROK = Republic of Korea; RHS = right-hand side.

Notes:

1. ASEAN+3 is defined to include member states of ASEAN plus the People's Republic of China; Hong Kong, China; Japan; and the Republic of Korea.
2. ASEAN comprises the markets of Cambodia, Indonesia, the Lao People's Democratic Republic, Malaysia, the Philippines, Singapore, Thailand, and Viet Nam.
3. The EU-20 includes European Union member markets Austria, Belgium, Croatia, Cyprus, Estonia, Finland, France, Germany, Greece, Ireland, Italy, Latvia, Lithuania, Luxembourg, Malta, the Netherlands, Portugal, Slovakia, Slovenia, and Spain.
4. Data include both local currency and foreign currency issues.

Source: *AsianBondsOnline* calculations based on Bloomberg LP data.

[16] The Herfindahl–Hirschman Index is a commonly accepted measure of market concentration. The index is used to measure market diversification and is calculated by summing the squared share of each type of sustainable bonds. A lower score indicates greater diversity.

Figure 12: Tenor Profiles of ASEAN+3 and European Union 20 Sustainable Bonds Outstanding by Type of Bond at the End of June 2025

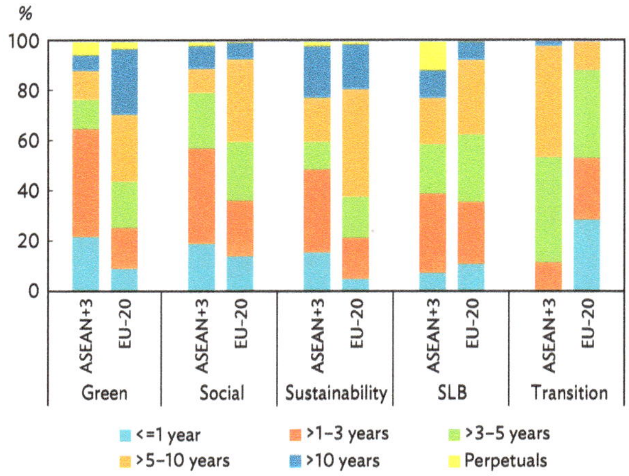

ASEAN+3 = Association of Southeast Asian Nations plus the People's Republic of China; Hong Kong, China; Japan; and the Republic of Korea; EU-20 = European Union 20; SLB = sustainability-linked bond.

Notes:
1. The EU-20 includes EU member markets Austria, Belgium, Croatia, Cyprus, Estonia, Finland, France, Germany, Greece, Ireland, Italy, Latvia, Lithuania, Luxembourg, Malta, the Netherlands, Portugal, Slovakia, Slovenia, and Spain.
2. Data include both local currency and foreign currency issues.
3. SLBs include transition-linked bonds.

Source: *AsianBondsOnline* computations based on Bloomberg LP data.

Figure 13: ASEAN+3 Sustainable Bond Issuance and Share of the Global Total

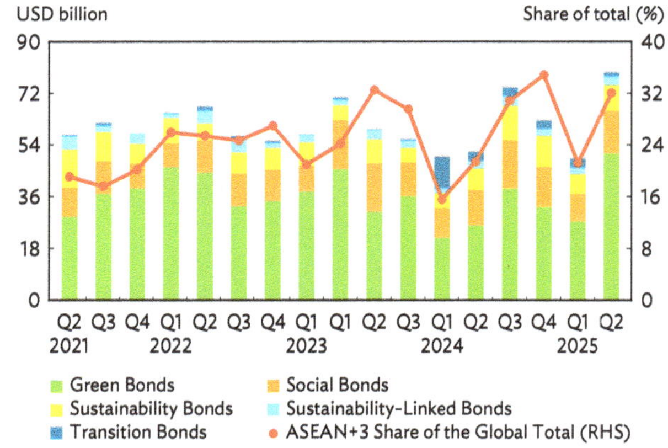

ASEAN+3 = Association of Southeast Asian Nations plus the People's Republic of China; Hong Kong, China; Japan; and the Republic of Korea; RHS = right-hand side; USD = United States dollar.

Notes:
1. Data include both local currency and foreign currency issues.
2. Sustainability-linked bonds include transition-linked bonds.

Source: *AsianBondsOnline* calculations based on Bloomberg LP data.

Figure 14: Market Profile of ASEAN+3 Sustainable Bond Issuance in the Second Quarter of 2025

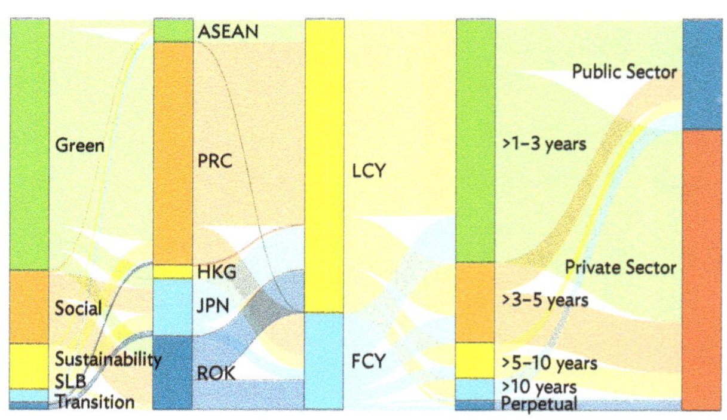

ASEAN = Association of Southeast Asian Nations; PRC = People's Republic of China; FCY = foreign currency; HKG = Hong Kong, China; JPN = Japan; ROK = Republic of Korea; LCY = local currency; SLB = sustainability-linked bond.

Notes:
1. ASEAN+3 is defined to include member states of ASEAN plus the People's Republic of China; Hong Kong, China; Japan; and the Republic of Korea.
2. ASEAN comprises the markets of Cambodia, Indonesia, Malaysia, the Philippines, Singapore, Thailand, and Viet Nam.
3. SLBs include transition-linked bonds.

Source: *AsianBondsOnline* calculations based on Bloomberg LP data.

market with 79.5% carrying tenors of 5 years or less, while transition bonds had the longest with 46.2% holding tenors of over 5 years (**Figure 12**).

Sustainable Bond Issuance

ASEAN+3's sustainable bond issuance totaled USD79.6 billion in Q2 2025 on growth of 60.6% q-o-q, following a 21.2% q-o-q contraction in the previous quarter. Growth in sustainable bond issuance in ASEAN+3 was the market's most rapid since Q2 2021 and also outpaced growth in both the EU-20 (23.1% q-o-q) and the global market (6.5% q-o-q). The increase in sustainable bond issuance was supported by improved investor sentiment amid ongoing monetary easing and progress in trade negotiations between the United States and major regional trading partners. During Q2 2025, ASEAN+3 accounted for 32.2% of total sustainable bond issuance worldwide, up from 21.4% in the previous quarter (**Figure 13**). Sustainable bond issuance accounted for 8.4% of ASEAN's total bond issuance in Q2 2025, exceeding the corresponding shares in the global market (4.7%) and ASEAN+3 (4.3%).

- Across bond types, green bonds comprised 64.8% of ASEAN+3's total sustainable bond issuance in Q2 2025, followed by social bonds (18.6%) (**Figure 14**). The PRC accounted for 57.2% of regional sustainable bond issuance and led green bond issuance by a wide margin (78.5% of the regional total). The Republic of Korea contributed 18.5% of ASEAN+3's sustainable bond issuance during the quarter and was the largest issuer of social bonds (62.1% of the regional total). ASEAN economies accounted for 6.1% of the regional sustainable bond issuance total, contributing a majority (52.8%) of sustainability-linked bonds.

- LCY financing accounted for 75.6% of ASEAN+3's sustainable bond issuance in Q2 2025, which was below the LCY issuance share of 95.0% in the region's general bond market and the corresponding share of 88.9% in the EU-20's sustainable bond market. Within ASEAN+3, the LCY financing share in Q2 2025 was highest in the ASEAN sustainable bond market at 99.5%, which also exceeded the corresponding share in ASEAN's general bond market (75.1%) (Figure 14).
- Bonds with maturities of 5 years or less accounted for 82.9% of ASEAN+3 sustainable bond issuance in Q2 2025. This was much higher than the corresponding shares of 31.5% in the EU-20 and 45.6% in ASEAN+3's general bond market. Bonds with tenors of 5 years or less accounted for 93.7% and 88.2% of sustainable bond issuance in the PRC and the Republic of Korea, respectively, while in ASEAN markets around 61.3% of sustainable bond issuance during the quarter carried a maturity of over 5 years—with more than half carrying a maturity longer than 10 years. Thus, the size-weighted average maturity of ASEAN sustainable bond issuance in Q2 2025 was 13.9 years, compared with 8.5 years in the EU-20 and 5.1 years in ASEAN+3. ASEAN's relatively longer average maturity was largely driven by a 29-year green bond issued by the Government of Singapore during the quarter.
- Corporate financing comprised 71.8% of ASEAN+3 sustainable bond issuance in Q2 2025, compared with a corresponding share of 38.5% in the region's general bond market (Figure 14). Higher shares of private sector sustainable bond issuance were most evident in large regional markets including the PRC (90.1%) and Japan (73.0%), while public sector financing was more prevalent among sustainable bond issuance in ASEAN markets (60.8%); the Republic of Korea (62.0%); and Hong Kong, China (96.8%). Within the private sector, financial firms were the most active issuers of sustainable bonds during the quarter with a share of 55.6%, followed by industrials (13.8%) and utilities (13.6%) (**Figure 15**). To promote more investment in renewable energy, policymakers need to foster a more enabling environment. **Box 2** explores various economic and noneconomic drivers of renewable energy investments.

Figure 15: ASEAN+3 Sustainable Bond Issuance by Sector in the Second Quarter of 2025

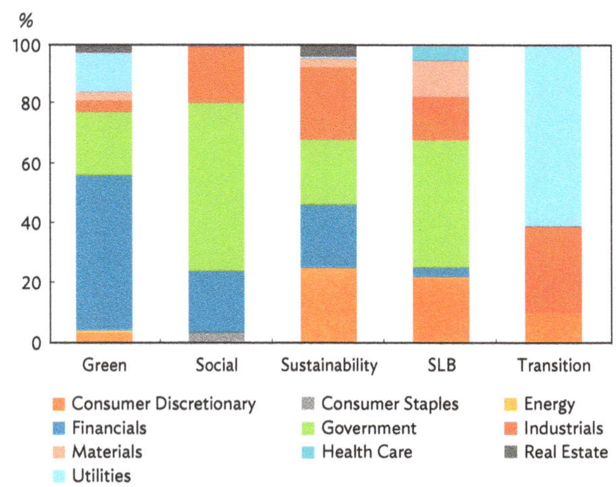

SLB = sustainability-linked bond.

Notes:
1. ASEAN+3 is defined to include member states of the Association of Southeast Asian Nations plus the People's Republic of China; Hong Kong, China; Japan; and the Republic of Korea.
2. Data include both local currency and foreign currency issues.
3. SLBs include transition-linked bonds.

Source: *AsianBondsOnline* computations based on Bloomberg LP data.

Box 2: Unlocking Renewable Energy Investments—The Role of Economic and Noneconomic Drivers

The global energy landscape is undergoing a profound transformation, driven by growing climate imperatives, the limited fossil fuel supply, and ongoing geopolitical uncertainties. Fossil fuels remain the dominant source of energy-related emissions globally, contributing to nearly 90% of carbon emissions worldwide. As a result, the transition to renewable energy (RE) is no longer a choice; it is a necessity. Beyond its environmental significance, RE is also essential for improving national energy security, tackling socioeconomic inequalities, and meeting the Paris Agreement target of limiting global warming to significantly below 2°C—ideally 1.5°C.

Despite the recognized urgency and promising growth in RE investments—currently estimated at USD2 trillion annually—this still falls substantially short of the USD5 trillion required to achieve net-zero carbon targets by mid-century (International Energy Agency 2022). This considerable investment gap represents a critical challenge to global sustainability efforts. This shortfall persists even in developed economies with mature financial systems, suggesting that the barriers to RE investment are not solely financial. Instead, it points to broader structural and institutional challenges embedded within national policies, market regulations, and investment frameworks.

Understanding what drives—or impedes—investment in RE is therefore vital. In this context, Uddin et al. (2025) explore the determinants of RE investments using a comprehensive panel dataset of 36 economies from 2000 to 2020. The analysis uses a comparative approach to assess both developed and developing economies, while categorizing factors into economic (e.g., industrial growth, environmental taxes, inflation, and oil prices) and noneconomic (e.g., social globalization, environmental technology, climate vulnerability, and political instability) dimensions. This approach helps uncover the potential structural differences between developing and developed economies, given the well-documented uneven distribution of RE investments worldwide. **Figure B2.1** illustrates that per capita RE investments are notably greater in developed economies compared to emerging and developing economies, albeit the People's Republic of China displays exceptionally considerable investments. This visual representation conveys the core premise for the study's comparative analysis and reinforces the necessity of a differentiated approach to policy recommendations.

Figure B2.1: Renewable Energy Investments per Capita

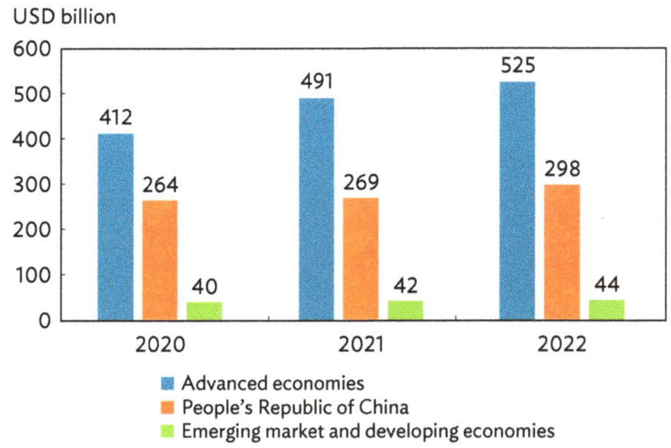

USD = United States dollar.

Note: Emerging market and developing economies exclude the People's Republic of China.

Source: International Energy Agency. 2022. *World Energy Investment 2022*.

Uddin et al. (2025) employ sophisticated econometric techniques to show a clear divergence between the two economic groups: In developed economies, industrial growth boosts RE investment, supporting green growth and clean technology; in developing economies, it has the opposite effect. Developing economies continue to depend significantly on fossil fuels to facilitate rapid industrialization, rendering the adoption of clean energy both financially and infrastructurally challenging. Moreover, the high up-front capital required for solar and wind projects, coupled with limited public financing and access to green credit, limits scalability in developing economies.

Environmental taxes emerge as a consistently positive driver of RE investment across both economic groups. Their effectiveness highlights the importance of policy instruments that make pollution-intensive energy more expensive relative to renewables. In contrast, inflation exerts a negative influence on RE investments in developed economies, where financial markets exhibit heightened sensitivity to increased interest rates and borrowing expenses. Inflation appears to

This box was written by Md. Bokhtiar Hasan (associate professor in the Department of Finance & Banking at Islamic University, Bangladesh) based on G.S. Uddin, B. Hasan, D. Park, S. Ali, and C. Wadstrom. 2025. Exploring the Economic and Non-Economic Determinants of Investments in Renewable Energy. *Renewable Energy*. 255. 123750.

continued on next page

Box 2 *continued*

have a weaker influence in developing economies, likely because RE projects there are often supported by public subsidies or fixed tariff structures that insulate them from short-term macroeconomic shocks.

Oil prices, often cited as a key determinant of the likelihood of energy transition, significantly and negatively influence RE investments only in developing economies. When oil prices rise, fossil fuels may become more attractive in the short term due to immediate affordability, especially in economies lacking strong energy infrastructure or subsidies for renewables.

Noneconomic factors increasingly influence RE investment decisions, often overshadowing economic factors. Social globalization—the increasing interconnectedness and interaction between people and groups across borders—emerges as a strong enabler of RE investments. In developed economies, it amplifies environmental awareness, facilitates technology transfer, and encourages public pressure for clean energy adoption. Even in developing economies, social globalization contributes positively, albeit more modestly.

Environmental-related technology shows a strong correlation with RE investments, particularly in developing economies. However, its influence presents a more nuanced picture in developed economies: a negative influence at lower investment levels but a positive effect at the highest quantile. This suggests that in mature RE markets, only large-scale, disruptive innovations or major R&D efforts drive new investment, whereas incremental improvements have limited impact. Therefore, technology policy in these economies should focus on breakthrough innovations and large demonstration projects to stimulate substantial RE investments.

Climate vulnerability also consistently drives RE investments across both economic groups. This highlights how greater exposure to climate risks directly motivates increased RE investments as an integral part of climate adaptation and resilience. By contrast, political instability significantly deters RE investments in developed economies, where investors rely on policy certainty and long-term commitments. Interestingly, its effect is not statistically significant in developing economies, likely because investors already factor such risks into their decision-making in these contexts. The impacts of economic and noneconomic factors on RE investments are summarized in **Figure B2.2**.

These findings offer three major takeaways for policy makers. First, the contrasting effects of key variables—such as industrial growth and inflation—between the two economy groups underline the need for tailored strategies. In this context, a universal policy approach is unlikely to be effective. Developing economies require support in overcoming cost and infrastructure barriers, while advanced economies need to focus on innovation and scaling.

Figure B2.2: Summary of Economic and Noneconomic Drivers of Renewable Energy Investments—Developed Versus Developing Economies

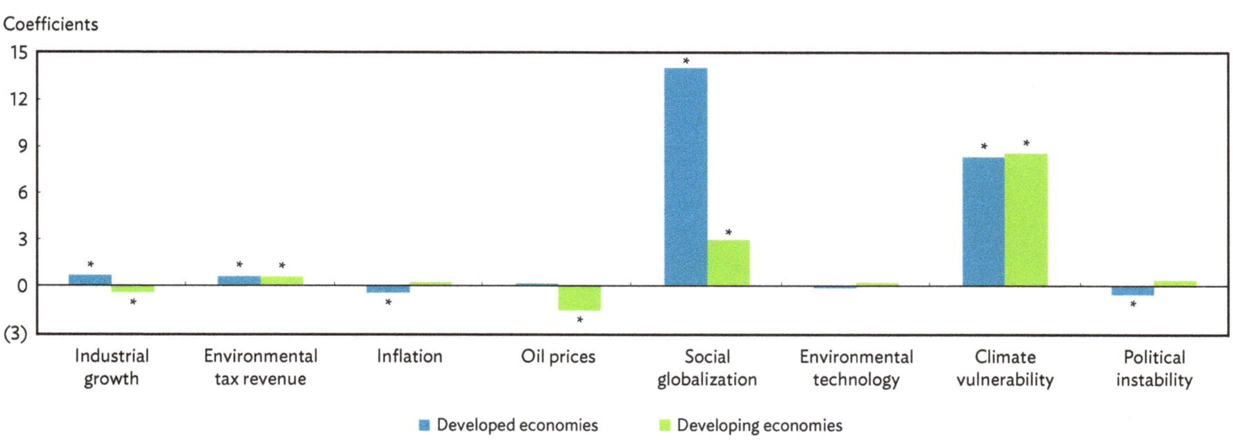

( ) = negative.

Note: * indicates statistical significance at the 5% level.

Source: G.S. Uddin, B. Hasan, D. Park, S. Ali, and C. Wadstrom. 2025. Exploring the Economic and Non-Economic Determinants of Investments in Renewable Energy. *Renewable Energy*. 255. 123750.

continued on next page

Box 2 *continued*

Second, the findings emphasize the need for policy makers to consider noneconomic factors. Economies that encourage education, social awareness, and digital integration are better positioned to build public support for clean energy transitions. This calls for a broader view of energy policy—one that incorporates societal and institutional dimensions alongside traditional economic instruments.

Third, even with supportive macroeconomic conditions, RE investments often stall without stable governance and institutional credibility. Strengthening the rule of law, reducing regulatory uncertainty, and aligning national strategies with long-term international climate goals can de-risk renewable infrastructure investments and attract global capital.

In the end, accelerating the global transition to RE necessitates a sophisticated understanding of diverse investment drivers and a steadfast commitment to context-specific, integrated policy frameworks that address the multifaceted economic and noneconomic factors at play.

References

International Energy Agency. 2022. *World Energy Investment 2022.*

G.S. Uddin, B. Hasan, D. Park, S. Ali, and C. Wadstrom. 2025. Exploring the Economic and Non-Economic Determinants of Investments in Renewable Energy. *Renewable Energy*. 255. 123750.

Policy and Regulatory Developments

People's Republic of China

The People's Republic of China Imposes Value-Added Tax on Certain Bond Types

The Ministry of Finance announced that bonds issued by the central government, local governments, and financial institutions would be charged a 6% value-added tax on interest starting 8 August. Existing bonds that were issued before 8 August are exempt from the value-added tax.

Hong Kong, China

Hong Kong Monetary Authority Enhances Offshore Renminbi Bond Repurchase Arrangements

On 8 July, the Hong Kong Monetary Authority announced two important enhancements to the offshore renminbi bond repurchase agreement (repo) business to facilitate the participation of Northbound Connect investors in repo transactions. First, the rehypothecation of bond collateral will be allowed during the repo period. Previously, the bond collateral was locked in and managed by the Central Money Markets Unit platform and could not be re-used during the repo period. Allowing the re-use of bond collateral will reduce financial costs and improve liquidity management for market participants. Second, cross-currency repo transactions using Hong Kong dollars, United States dollars, and euros will be supported. Currently, offshore repo transactions can only be settled in Chinese yuan. Allowing settlements in these other currencies will further enhance participants' liquidity management. The two improvements, which take effect on 25 August, are in line with international market best practices.

Indonesia

Indonesia's Ministry of Finance Revises 2025 Budget Deficit Estimate

In July, the Ministry of Finance of Indonesia revised its fiscal outlook for 2025, with the budget deficit now estimated to reach 2.78% of gross domestic product (GDP), up from an earlier estimate of 2.53%. The revision was needed to help support the government's key programs amid ongoing volatility in the global economy. In the first 6 months of the year, the budget deficit reached IDR204 trillion or the equivalent of 0.8% of GDP. The wider budget deficit (IDR662 trillion) for the full year 2025 was partly due to lower revenue collections in the first half of the year. The Ministry of Finance plans to use excess funds and savings from the 2024 budget to avoid issuing more debt.

Indonesia Issues Its First Orange Bond

On 9 July, the first orange bond in Indonesia was issued by Permodalan Nasional Madan, an Indonesian state-owned microfinance institution. Orange bonds are sustainable bonds meant to support gender equality. The issuance amounted to IDR1.0 trillion of conventional orange bonds, which comprised 370-day, 3-year, and 5-year tranches. The company also issued the first orange *sukuk* (Islamic bond) amounting to IDR1.8 trillion and consisting of similar maturities.

Republic of Korea

The Republic of Korea Announces Second Supplementary Budget Proposal

In June, the new administration in the Republic of Korea announced this year's second supplementary budget proposal totaling KRW30.5 trillion: KRW15.2 trillion for economic stimulus, KRW5.0 trillion for livelihood stability projects, and the remaining KRW10.3 trillion for revenue adjustments as the government expects a shortfall for the year. The main highlight of the economic stimulus is the distribution of livelihood recovery coupons

(KRW10.3 trillion) and additional consumption incentives (KRW1.0 trillion). Other economic measures include supporting the construction sector, small and medium-sized enterprises, and AI and renewable energy industries, as well as a debt restructuring program for small business owners. On 6 July, the National Assembly approved the proposal and raised the amount to KRW31.8 trillion. The government plans to issue KRW21.1 trillion worth of government bonds to partially fund the supplementary budget, resulting in an increase in the fiscal-deficit-to-GDP ratio from 3.6% in 2024 to 4.2% in 2025.

Malaysia

Ministry of Economy Releases the 13th Malaysian Plan to Boost Economic Growth

On 31 July, the Ministry of Economy released the 13th Malaysian Plan (13MP), outlining an annual development expenditure allocation of MYR86.0 billion for 2026–2030, up from an annual average of MYR79.0 billion during 2021–2024. The 13MP targets annual GDP growth in 2026–2030 of 4.5%–5.5%, compared with 5.2% average annual growth in 2021–2024. The 13MP directs the government to spend at least 3.0% of GDP every year on development expenditure, more than half of which (52.8%) is focused on boosting economic growth. The 13MP also aims to reduce the fiscal deficit to below 3.0% of GDP by 2030, down from 4.1% in 2024. These actions are key to reducing the government's debt load, which was at 64.6% of GDP at the end of 2024, up from 52.4% in 2019.

Philippines

The Philippines Trims Its Treasury Bond Auction Plan for the Third Quarter of 2025

In June, the Bureau of the Treasury reduced its planned Treasury auctions for the third quarter (Q3) of 2025 by PHP45.0 billion to PHP690.0 billion, primarily by scaling back the sale of Treasury bonds. While planned issuance of Treasury bills remained steady at PHP325.0 billion, planned issuance of Treasury bonds totaled PHP365.0 billion, reflecting a 12.3% drop from the previous quarter's PHP410.0 billion. The Q3 2025 borrowing plan comprises 47.1% Treasury bills and 52.9% Treasury bonds, representing 27.1% of the government's total borrowing target of PHP2.6 trillion for 2025. In addition to the PHP690.0 billion Treasury auction plan, the government also intends to issue Retail Treasury Bonds worth around PHP200.0 billion in Q3 2025.

GCash Launches Access to Philippine Government Securities

On 24 July, GCash—an e-wallet mobile platform—launched its GBonds feature that allows fully verified users to invest in government securities even without a bank account. GBonds is offering Treasury bills for a minimum investment of PHP500 and Retail Treasury Bonds for a minimum investment of PHP5,000. The GBonds feature is powered by the Philippine Digital Asset Exchange and Bonds.ph in partnership with the Bureau of the Treasury. This initiative seeks to broaden the government securities' investor base and promote financial inclusion to small investors.

Singapore

Monetary Authority of Singapore and People's Bank of China to Strengthen Green and Transition Finance

On 11 July, the Monetary Authority of Singapore and the People's Bank of China met to strengthen their collaboration through the Singapore–China Green Finance Taskforce. This initiative smoothens cross-border deals by allowing firms in both Singapore and the PRC to issue green bonds in compliance with a shared international standard. The taskforce also collaborates with the Singapore Exchange and the China International Capital Corporation to facilitate the "Green Corridor" to further encourage cross-border green finance flows, with a focus on issuances of green panda bonds in its initial phases. Singapore's CapitaLand Investment's previous issuance of a 3-year sustainability-linked panda bond worth CNY1.0 billion jump-started this collaborative initiative, setting a path for further similar issuances.

Thailand

Bank of Thailand Adds Banks to the Local Currency Transaction Framework

On 5 August, the Bank of Thailand, along with Bank Negara Malaysia and Bank Indonesia, announced the appointment of additional commercial banks to participate in the harmonized local currency transaction framework across Thailand, Malaysia, and Indonesia. Qualified commercial banks, called appointed cross-currency dealers, will facilitate cross-border settlement of trade and investment across the three markets. The expanded network of commercial banks will enhance market access to local currency liquidity and provide market participants with more options for cross-border transactions.

Viet Nam

Corporate Bond Private Placements Capped at Five Times Issuer's Equity

In June, the Government of Viet Nam enacted Article 128 of the 2025 Amended Law on Enterprises, requiring a debt-to-equity ratio limit for corporate bond issuers via private placements. Effective 1 July, this new regulation mandates that nonpublic companies will only be permitted to issue corporate bonds through private placements if their total liabilities—including the value of the proposed bond issuance—do not exceed five times their equity, as disclosed in their audited financial statements from the year preceding the bond issuance. This leverage cap does not apply to entities that are already governed by more stringent issuance conditions under specialized laws such as state-owned enterprises, credit institutions, real estate firms, insurers, and securities firms. The new regulation aims to strengthen investor protection and avoid systemic risks in Viet Nam's corporate bond market.

How Sovereign Sustainable Bond Issuance Shakes Up the Corporate Sustainable Bond Market: Evidence from Developing Asian Markets

Motivation

Asian economies have large populations and face key social and environmental development challenges. Sustainable finance has become critical to achieving environmental and social goals across the world. The global sustainable bond market reached a size of USD5.0 trillion in 2024, with Asia accounting for 21% of total bonds outstanding. However, the share of sustainable bonds in Asia's total bond market (2.3%) remains significantly below that of the European Union (EU) (8.2%). Given the region's fiscal constraints, enhancing private sector participation in sustainable finance is imperative to advance sustainable development. While sovereign sustainable bond issuance is growing in Asia overall, the share of sovereign issuance in sustainable bond markets is still relatively small compared to the EU.

The issuance of sovereign sustainable bonds not only finances environmentally and socially beneficial projects but can also contribute to the expansion of private sustainable bond financing by signaling government commitment, establishing taxonomies and reporting standards, and providing pricing benchmarks. While the importance of sovereign bonds in corporate bond market development is well established, empirical evidence on sovereign sustainable bonds' implications for corporate sustainable bond markets remains underexplored. Only a few studies highlight channels such as demonstration effects, investor confidence, and government signaling (see, for example, Cheng, Ehlers, and Packer 2022; Cheng et al. 2024), but systematic evidence remains scarce.

Focusing on eight developing Asian markets—Hong Kong, China; India; Indonesia; the Republic of Korea; Malaysia; the Philippines; Singapore; and Thailand—this study investigates whether and how sovereign sustainable bond issuance affects the liquidity and pricing dynamics of corporate sustainable bond markets.[17] This study aims to (i) assess the impact of sovereign sustainable bond issuance on the liquidity (bid–ask spread) and yield spread of corporate sustainable bonds, (ii) examine the mechanisms through which sovereign issuance affects corporate sustainable bond markets, and (iii) provide evidence-based insights to inform public policy strategies in deepening sustainable finance in Asia. This study contributes to the literature by deepening our understanding of the role of sovereign sustainable bonds in scaling private sustainable finance.

Sample and Method

The study constructs a panel dataset of corporate sustainable bond data from 2018 to 2024. Empirically, this study adopts the panel vector autoregression model to estimate the interactions between sovereign sustainable bond issuance and the pricing dynamics of corporate sustainable bonds. The key dependent variables are (i) bid–ask spreads of corporate sustainable bonds, which capture liquidity; and (ii) yield spreads between corporate sustainable bonds and government bonds of the same denominating currency and tenor. The key independent variable of interest is sovereign sustainable bond issuance, captured by a dummy variable for a sovereign sustainable bond issuance debut, which refers to when the first sovereign sustainable bond was issued in an economy.

This special section is an executive summary of a research paper in the *Asian Economic Policy Review* titled "How Sovereign Sustainable Bond Issuance Shakes Up the Corporate Sustainable Bond Market: Evidence from Asian Markets." This special section was written by the coauthors of the aforementioned paper, Seiwan Kim (professor at Ewha Womans University and president at Korea Capital Market Institute) and Sunjoo Yang (PhD candidate at Ewha Womans University), and by Resi Ong Olivares (consultant), Donghyun Park (economic advisor), and Shu (Grace) Tian (principal economist) at the Asian Development Bank, Manila.

17 Each of these markets has issued sovereign sustainable bonds.

To understand the sources of reaction of corporate sustainable bond yield spreads to the first sovereign sustainable bond issuance in a market, this study further decomposed yield spreads into (i) a "greenium" to capture the yield difference between a sustainable corporate bond and a conventional reference corporate bond with similar pricing attributes (e.g., rating, tenor, and denominating currency); and (ii) a risk premium that measures the yield difference between the reference conventional corporate bond and government bond with the same tenor and denominating currency. The study further investigates the possible working channel through which a sovereign sustainable bond issuance influences a corporate sustainable bond market by assessing (i) supply side changes in corporate sustainable bond markets after the first sovereign sustainable bond issuance, and (ii) the demand for sustainable assets, proxied by flows into environmental, social, and governance mutual funds after the first sovereign sustainable bond issuance.

Key Findings

Liquidity

The debut of sovereign sustainable bond issuance leads to a short-run improvement in corporate sustainable bond liquidity, as reflected in narrower bid–ask spreads. As shown in **Table 2**, the effect becomes significant as the horizon lengthens, indicating that liquidity gains are not short-lived but cumulative. Monthly and quarterly data allow for more significant liquidity improvement to accumulate over time. However, liquidity improvement affected by a single sovereign sustainable bond issuance cannot be sustained as investors adjust their portfolios, which requires deeper investor participation and greater market depth.

Table 2: Dynamic Properties of Sovereign Sustainable Bond Introduction on Bid–Ask Spreads

	Daily	Monthly	Quarterly
Short-run effect	-0.0003 (0.0002)	-0.0048* (0.0025)	-0.0232*** (0.0087)
Long-run effect	-0.0110	-0.0859	-0.1255
Mean lag	5.3 days	4.9 days	7.5 days

Notes: The values in parentheses are heteroskedasticity robust standard errors. * and *** represent significance at the 10% and 1% levels, respectively.

Source: Kim, S., R. Olivares, D. Park, S. Tian, and S. Yang. 2025. How Sovereign Sustainable Bond Issuance Shakes Up the Corporate Sustainable Bond Market? Evidence from Asian Markets. *Asian Economic Policy Review*.

Yield Spread

Our findings indicate that sovereign sustainable bond issuance reduces corporate sustainable bond yield spreads over the medium term (**Figure 16**). Similar to the liquidity evidence, the effect on yield spreads is not immediate but becomes statistically significant in the monthly and quarterly models, reflecting the gradual pricing in of the possible signaling and demonstration effects of sovereign sustainable bonds, which strengthens investor confidence and builds demand for sustainable assets. Yield spreads also display strong autoregressive dynamics, confirming that price adjustments in bond markets unfold gradually. Overall, the results imply that sovereign sustainable bonds contribute to lowering corporate sustainable bond financing costs over time.

Figure 16: Impact of Sovereign Sustainable Bond Issuance on Corporate Yield Spreads, Greeniums, and Risk Premiums

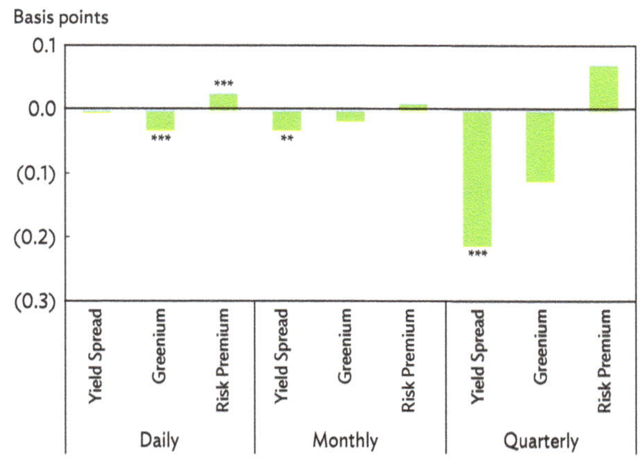

( ) = negative.

Note: ** and *** represent significance at the 5% and 1% levels, respectively.

Source: Kim, S., R. Olivares, D. Park, S. Tian, and S. Yang. 2025. How Sovereign Sustainable Bond Issuance Shakes Up the Corporate Sustainable Bond Market? Evidence from Asian Markets. *Asian Economic Policy Review*.

To examine the sources of the decline in yield spreads, we decompose them into a greenium and a risk premium. The results in Figure 16 show that improvement in the yield spread over the medium term is mostly driven by a lower greenium, which echoes improved investor sentiment and stronger demand for sustainable bonds following sovereign issuance. In contrast, the risk premium rises in the short run, reflecting liquidity adjustments and temporary portfolio rebalancing away from conventional reference corporate bonds, but this impact fades over the medium horizon. This suggests that the lasting impact of sovereign issuance operates mainly through the greenium.

Underlying Mechanisms

Increased supply and demand contribute to enhanced liquidity and reduced financing costs in corporate sustainable bond markets.

- On the supply side, a sovereign sustainable bond issuance debut leads to a higher share of sustainable bond issuance in corporate bonds, more unique issuers, greater market diversity in terms of sectors and issuers, and longer financing maturities in the corporate sustainable bond market (**Figure 17**). These outcomes suggest that sovereign issuance helps broaden and deepen corporate sustainable bond market participation.
- On the demand side, evidence shows an increase in fund inflows into exchange-traded environmental, social, and governance funds following the sovereign sustainable bond issuance debut, reflecting greater investor interest in broad sustainable assets (i.e., passive, rather than active, trading) (**Figure 18**).

Figure 17: Impact of Sovereign Sustainable Bond Issuance Debut on the Supply of Corporate Sustainable Bonds

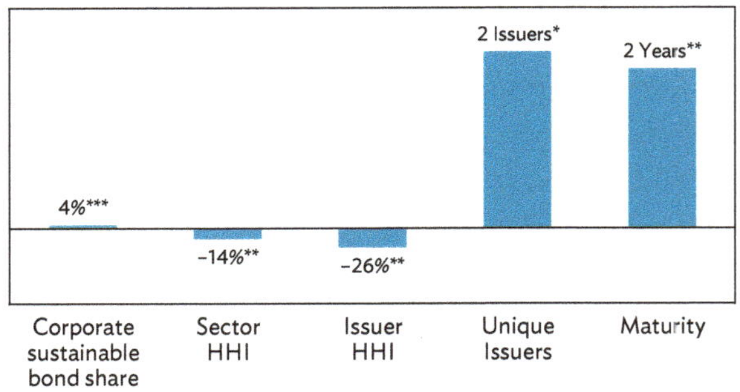

HHI = Herfindahl–Hirschman Index.

Notes: The corporate sustainable bond share is the amount of corporate sustainable bond issuance relative to total corporate bond issuance during the quarter. The HHI is a commonly accepted measure of market concentration. The index is used to measure the investor profile diversification of the region's local currency bond market and is calculated by summing the squared share of each investor group in the bond market. Maturity is the size-weighted maturity in years of sustainable bonds issuance. *, **, and *** represent significance at the 10%, 5%, and 1% levels, respectively.

Source: Kim, S., R. Olivares, D. Park, S. Tian, and S. Yang. 2025. How Sovereign Sustainable Bond Issuance Shakes Up the Corporate Sustainable Bond Market? Evidence from Asian Markets. *Asian Economic Policy Review*.

Policy Implications

The study yields some useful policy implications. Above all, it suggests that governments can effectively foster private sustainable finance with the issuance of sovereign sustainable bonds, which can promote pricing efficiency and lower financing costs in sustainable bond markets. Sovereign issuances act as a powerful signal of commitment to sustainable finance by boosting market confidence, as sovereign sustainable bonds help reduce related policy uncertainty and assure investors. Sovereign issuances can also boost supply and promote market development by setting pricing benchmarks, enhancing reporting transparency, defining sustainable bond standards and taxonomies, and providing demonstration effects.

Figure 18: Impact of Sovereign Sustainable Bond Issuance Debut on Demand for Corporate Sustainable Bonds

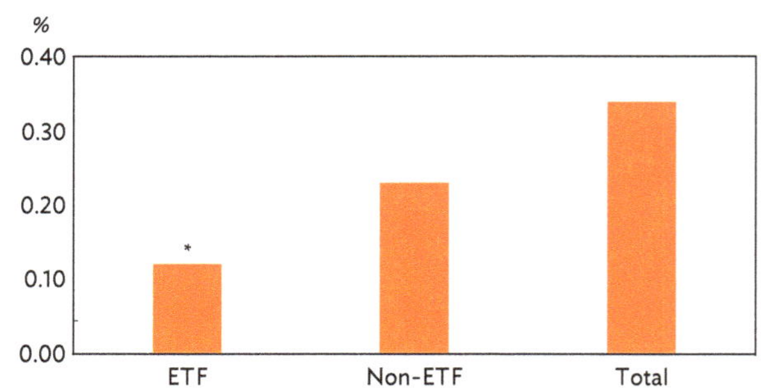

ETF = exchange-traded fund.

Notes: Total refers to net inflows into environmental, social, and governance (ESG) funds investing in sample markets from global sources, scaled by the funds' total net assets. It is broken down into inflows to exchange-traded ESG funds and non-exchange-traded ESG funds, each scaled by their respective net assets. * represents significance at the 10% level.

Source: Kim, S., R. Olivares, D. Park, S. Tian, and S. Yang. 2025. How Sovereign Sustainable Bond Issuance Shakes Up the Corporate Sustainable Bond Market? Evidence from Asian Markets. *Asian Economic Policy Review*.

To maximize the catalyzing impact, governments should adopt an integrated policy design that complements sovereign sustainable bond issuance with robust regulatory frameworks and fiscal incentives for issuers to mobilize private capital. The policy implications are relevant for emerging markets around the world. Evidence from developing Asia, where sustainable bonds account for a small fraction of the general bond market, implies that in all global emerging markets where sustainable bond markets are underdeveloped, governments can strategically use sovereign participation to scale up private sustainable finance and, more broadly, the development of bond markets and sustainable finance.

References

Cheng, G., T. Ehlers, and F. Packer. 2022. Sovereigns and Sustainable Bonds: Challenges and New Options. *BIS Quarterly Review*. September. pp. 47–56.

Cheng, G., T. Ehlers, F. Packer, and Y. Xiao. 2024. Sovereign Green Bonds: A Catalyst for Sustainable Debt market Development?" *International Monetary Fund Working Paper*. No. WP/24/120.

Kim, S., R. Olivares, D. Park, S. Tian, and S. Yang. 2025. How Sovereign Sustainable Bond Issuance Shakes Up the Corporate Sustainable Bond Market? Evidence from Asian Markets. *Asian Economic Policy Review*.

Market Summaries

People's Republic of China

Yield Movements

The People's Republic of China's (PRC) yield curve steepened between 2 June and 29 August. On average, bond yields declined by 9 basis points for tenors of 3 years or less, while they gained 9 basis points for tenors of 4 years or more (**Figure 1**). The steepening was due to improved sentiment, despite some weaker economic data, over easing tensions in the PRC–United States (US) trade dispute and continued government support measures. Investors rotating funds from bonds into stocks following the PRC–US trade pause extension also added upward pressure on long-term yields. Gains in the stock market were fueled by government calls to prioritize local chip makers and reports of an update to DeepSeek's AI model. Gross domestic product grew 5.2% year-on-year (y-o-y) in the second quarter (Q2) of 2025, slightly above the market expectation of a 5.1% y-o-y expansion but down from 5.4% y-o-y growth in the previous quarter. Retail sales growth declined to 3.7% y-o-y in July from 4.8% y-o-y in June, and industrial production also moderated to 5.7% y-o-y from 6.8% y-o-y during the same period. Despite the weakening, the *Asian Development Outlook July 2025* forecasts for the PRC remained unchanged from April at 4.7% for 2025 and 4.3% for 2026.

Figure 1: The People's Republic of China's Benchmark Yield Curve—Local Currency Government Bonds

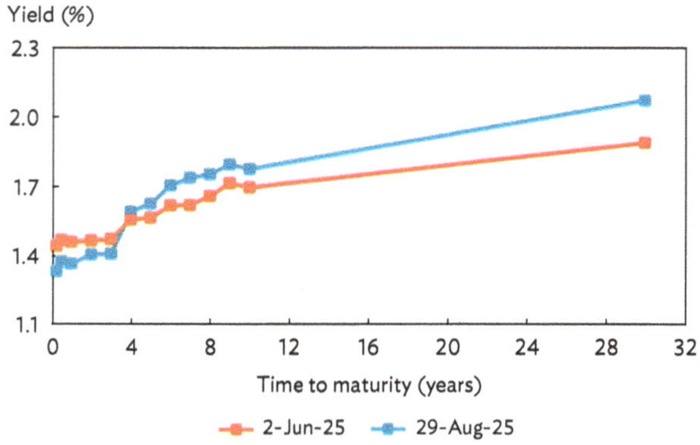

Source: Based on data from Bloomberg LP.

Local Currency Bond Market Size and Issuance

The PRC's local currency (LCY) bond market grew to a size of CNY165.3 trillion at the end of June, supported by expansions in both the government and corporate segments. Total bond market growth accelerated to 3.5% quarter-on-quarter (q-o-q) in Q2 2025 from 3.0% q-o-q in the prior quarter, buoyed by increased issuance during the period amid government stimulus measures announced in March (e.g., raising the budget deficit limit from 3% in 2024 to 4% in 2025) (**Figure 2**). Outstanding government bonds rose 3.9% q-o-q to CNY 113.8 trillion, matching the previous quarter's

Figure 2: Composition of Local Currency Bonds Outstanding in the People's Republic of China

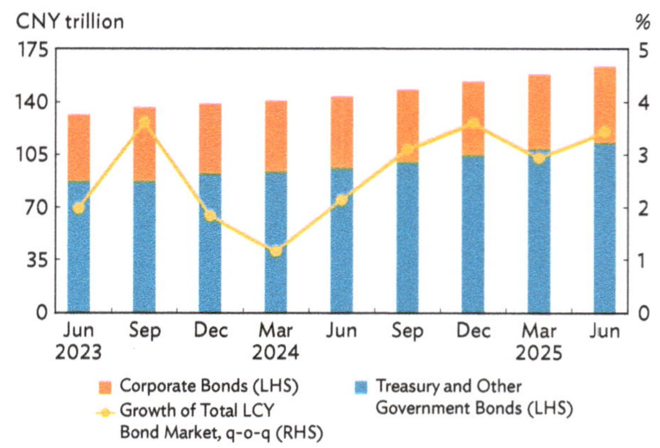

CNY = Chinese yuan, LCY = local currency, LHS = left-hand side, q-o-q = quarter-on-quarter, RHS = right-hand side.
Source: CEIC Data Company.

This market summary was written by Russ Jason Lo, consultant, Economic Research and Development Impact Department, Asian Development Bank, Manila.

growth, as rising issuance was largely offset by the large volume of bond maturities—total maturities were up by CNY1.3 trillion over the previous quarter.

Meanwhile, the corporate bond segment's expansion accelerated to 2.5% q-o-q from 1.0% q-o-q in the previous quarter on increased issuance in both the financial and nonfinancial sectors as borrowing costs declined. The Government of the PRC has also been conscious of risks building up in the economy. In addition to strengthening banks and local government finances, a *Financial Times* article noted that lower-rated corporate issuances have fallen as the PRC seeks to limit credit risk. (The article also raised the possibility that ratings on new issues may be inflated.) In addition, the PRC is allowing more foreign companies to issue bonds to improve the credit profile of the bond market, while foreign companies will benefit through lower yuan borrowing costs. The issuance of panda bonds, a CNY-denominated debt securities issued by overseas entities in the PRC that serve as a vital financing channel for international institutions, rose by 24.8% q-o-q and 7.1% y-o-y in Q2 2025 to CNY49.6 billion. The increase was due to a combination of several factors, including continued government initiatives to boost panda bonds, lower borrowing costs versus the US dollar, and greater investor interest in CNY-denominated assets.

The PRC's bond issuance rebounded in Q2 2025, rising 23.2% q-o-q to CNY14.8 trillion. Government bond issuance growth strengthened to 19.7% q-o-q in Q2 2025 from 6.3% q-o-q in the prior quarter after the central government started issuing special Treasury bonds in March (**Figure 3**). The issuance of special Treasury bonds will be used to help fund government stimulus measures to support the economy. In addition, some of the debt raised will be used to help recapitalize state-owned banks. Corporate bond issuance was up due to increased capital-raising activities from banks amid economic uncertainty and stronger issuance from nonfinancials due to lower interest rates. Corporates have been shifting away from the issuance of G3 bonds over rising borrowing costs resulting from the wait-and-see stance of major advanced economy central banks.[18] G3 issuance in the PRC declined 13.7% q-o-q to USD26.9 billion in Q2 2025. There was a noticeable decline of 80.2% q-o-q in G3 currency bond issuance from real estate companies given the challenging

Figure 3: Composition of Local Currency Bond Issuance in the People's Republic of China

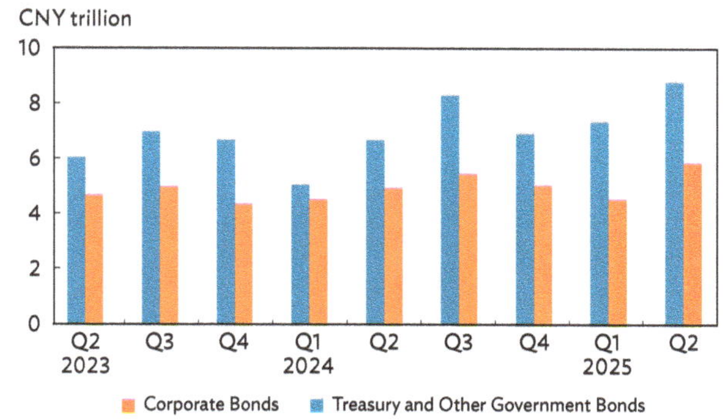

CNY = Chinese yuan, Q1 = first quarter, Q2 = second quarter, Q3 = third quarter, Q4 = fourth quarter.

Source: CEIC Data Company.

environment in the property sector, specifically an increasing number of defaults. In contrast, intraregional issuance from the PRC surged to USD1.5 billion in Q2 2025 from USD0.1 billion in the previous quarter.[19]

Investor Profile

Banks continued to be the largest holding group of Treasury bonds at the end of June. However, there was a decline in banks' holdings share to 67.1% from 70.4% a year earlier (**Figure 4**). The decline was partly due to banks limiting additional investments in the bond market following calls for caution from the central bank over

Figure 4: Investor Profile of Treasury Bonds

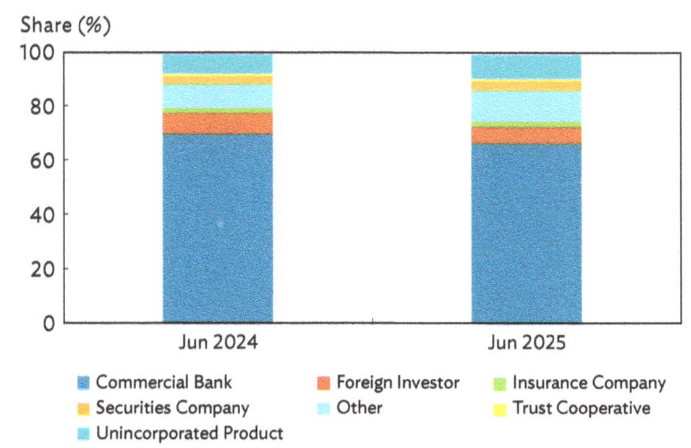

Source: CEIC Data Company.

[18] G3 currency bonds are denominated in either euros, Japanese yen, or United States dollars.

[19] Intra-regional bond issuance is defined as emerging East Asian bond issuance denominated in a regional currency excluding the issuer's home currency.

potential interest rate risks. A report by Caixin noted that local regulators have spoken to some rural banks over their bond investments.

Sustainable Bond Market

The PRC continued to lead the green bond market in emerging East Asia.[20] Green bonds dominate the PRC's sustainable bond market with a share of 86.8% (**Figure 5**). S&P Global noted that the PRC's strong issuance of green bonds is consistent with market efforts to transition to a low-carbon environment. According to the International Energy Agency, the PRC accounted for 35% of global greenhouse gas emissions in 2023. In addition, while the PRC released regulator guidelines for the issuance of green bonds in 2016, guidelines for a pilot program for social and sustainable bonds were only released in 2021. However, the PRC's green bonds carry relatively short-term tenors, with the share of bonds with remaining tenors of 5 years or less at 87.5%; shorter maturities can pose a challenge to funding long-term projects.

Figure 5: Market Profile of Outstanding Sustainable Bonds in the People's Republic of China at the End of June 2025

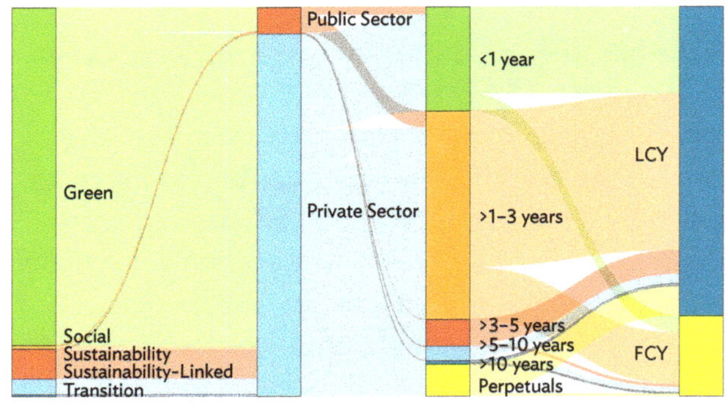

FCY = foreign currency, LCY = local currency.
Source: *AsianBondsOnline* calculations based on Bloomberg LP data.

20 Emerging East Asia is defined to include member states of the Association of Southeast Asian Nations plus the People's Republic of China; Hong Kong, China; and the Republic of Korea.

Hong Kong, China

Yield Movements

Between 2 June and 29 August, local currency (LCY) government bond yields in Hong Kong, China edged up for most maturities. Bond yields gained an average of 86 basis points for all maturities except the 10-year bond, which inched down by 5 basis points (**Figure 1**). The rise in bond yields was driven largely by a decline in the aggregate balance—a measure of interbank funding—following a series of interventions by the Hong Kong Monetary Authority to support the Hong Kong dollar's peg to the United States dollar. The aggregate balance decreased from HKD173.4 billion to HKD54.1 billion during the review period as the Hong Kong Monetary Authority purchased a total of HKD120.0 billion (in exchange for USD15.3 billion) from June to mid-August. The interventions drained excess funds from the financial system and pushed up borrowing costs, exerting upward pressure on bond yields. Meanwhile, inflation moderated to 1.0% year-on-year in July from 1.4% year-on-year in June as price pressures from domestic and external factors eased.

Figure 1: Hong Kong, China's Benchmark Yield Curve—Local Currency Government Bonds

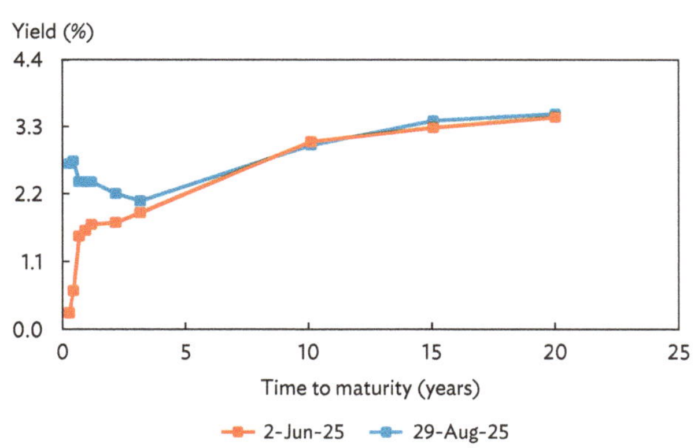

Source: Based on data from Bloomberg LP.

Local Currency Bond Market Size and Issuance

Growth in Hong Kong, China's LCY bonds outstanding slowed in the second quarter (Q2) of 2025, with the market reaching a size of HKD3,309.6 billion at the end of June. LCY bonds outstanding grew 2.0% quarter-on-quarter (q-o-q) in Q2 2025, down from 3.8% q-o-q in the preceding quarter (**Figure 2**). The weaker growth was driven by a contraction in government bonds and the slower expansion of corporate bonds. Hong Kong Special Administrative Region (HKSAR) government bonds declined 4.9% q-o-q in Q2 2025 after a modest rise of 1.8% q-o-q in the previous quarter, while growth in corporate bonds moderated to 4.4% q-o-q from 6.6% q-o-q. HKSAR government bonds contracted due to maturities outpacing issuance, while the expansion in corporate bonds decelerated as economic uncertainties capped issuance. Outstanding corporate bonds (HKD1,690.4 billion) comprised 51.1% of the LCY bond market at the end of June, while Exchange Fund Bills and Notes (HKD1,325.3 billion) and HKSAR bonds (HKD293.9 billion) accounted for the remaining 40.0% and 8.9%, respectively.

Figure 2: Composition of Local Currency Bonds Outstanding in Hong Kong, China

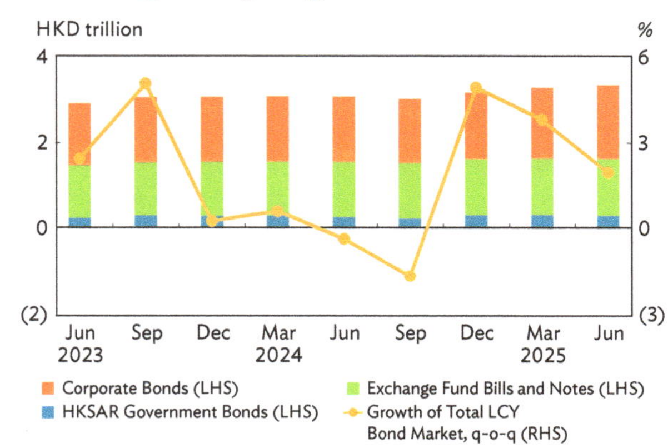

( ) = negative, HKD = Hong Kong dollar, HKSAR = Hong Kong Special Administrative Region, LCY = local currency, LHS = left-hand side, q-o-q = quarter-on-quarter, RHS = right-hand side.
Source: Hong Kong Monetary Authority.

This market summary was written by Debbie Gundaya, consultant, Economic Research and Development Impact Department, Asian Development Bank, Manila.

Total LCY bond sales rebounded in Q2 2025, boosted by increased issuance from the public sector. New issuance of LCY bonds grew 3.2% q-o-q to HKD1,446.3 billion in Q2 2025, reversing the 0.3% q-o-q decline in the previous quarter (**Figure 3**). Issuance of new HKSAR government bonds jumped 80.0% q-o-q to HKD13.5 billion and included a 30-year bond, the longest maturity of HKD-denominated HKSAR government bonds issued to date. Issuance of Exchange Fund Bills and Notes inched up to 1.0% q-o-q in Q2 2025 from 0.4% q-o-q in the prior quarter. Meanwhile, growth in the issuance of corporate bonds moderated to 8.1% q-o-q in Q2 2025 from 24.1% q-o-q as economic uncertainty dampened business sentiment. The top nonbank corporate issuer in Q2 2025 was Hong Kong Mortgage Corporation, which issued a total of HKD11.8 billion, or 56.8% of aggregate nonbank corporate bond issuance during the quarter.

Figure 3: Composition of Local Currency Bond Issuance in Hong Kong, China

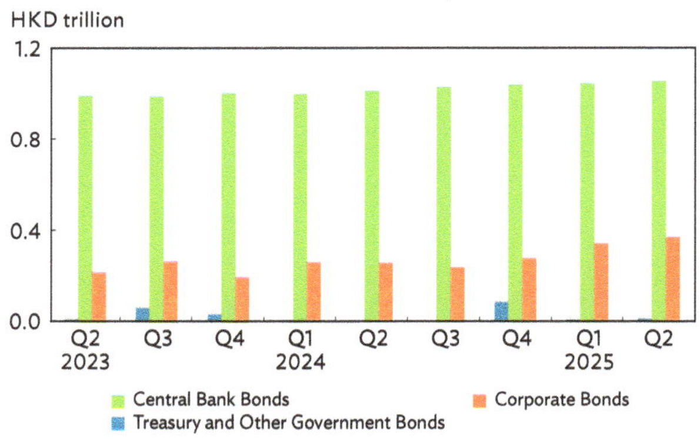

HKD = Hong Kong dollar, Q1 = first quarter, Q2 = second quarter, Q3 = third quarter, Q4 = fourth quarter.

Source: Hong Kong Monetary Authority.

Sustainable Bond Market

Hong Kong, China's sustainable bonds outstanding reached USD45.9 billion at the end of June and continued to mostly consist of green bonds. The stock of sustainable bonds fell 1.5% q-o-q in Q2 2025 due to the volume of maturities outpacing issuance. Green bonds continued to dominate the market with a 78.8% share, followed by social bonds with a 13.5% share (**Figure 4**). Public sector issuance again comprised a majority share of the outstanding sustainable bond market at the end of June, although its share declined to 56.7% from 58.2% at the end of March. While government bonds outstanding solely comprised green bonds, corporate bonds were slightly more diverse. About half of private sector securities were green bonds and a little under a third were social bonds. Bonds with tenors up to 5 years comprised 67.5% of outstanding securities at the end of June, resulting in a size-weighted average tenor of 4.7 years. About 81% of outstanding sustainable bonds were denominated in foreign currencies, which remained among the highest shares in emerging East Asia.[21] New issuance in Q2 2025 consisted of green bonds denominated in foreign currencies from the public sector and green bonds denominated in Hong Kong dollars from the private sector.

Figure 4: Market Profile of Outstanding Sustainable Bonds in Hong Kong, China at the End of June 2025

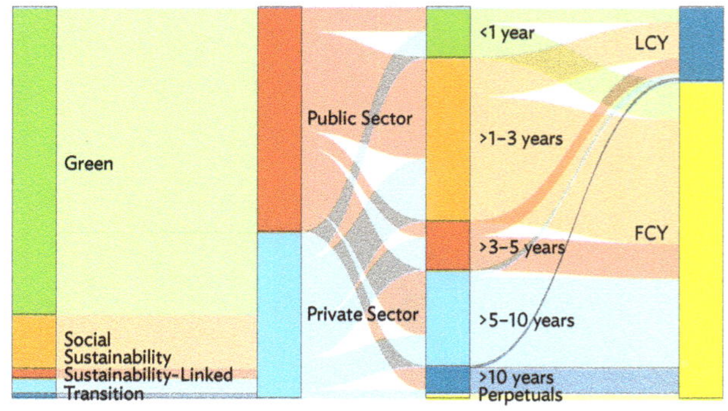

FCY = foreign currency, LCY = local currency.

Source: *AsianBondsOnline* calculations based on Bloomberg LP data.

21 Emerging East Asia is defined to include member states of the Association of Southeast Asian Nations plus the People's Republic of China; Hong Kong, China; and the Republic of Korea.

Indonesia

Yield Movements

The local currency (LCY) government bond yield curve in Indonesia shifted downward from 2 June to 29 August, largely influenced by monetary policy easing to boost economic growth amid low inflation expectations. During the review period, government bond yields declined across the curve, shedding an average of 55 basis points (**Figure 1**). The overall decline in yields was largely driven by the continued monetary easing stance of Bank Indonesia, which reduced its policy rate at both its 15–16 July and 19–20 August meetings by 25 basis points each to 5.00%. Bank Indonesia also hinted that there was further scope for rate cuts given the need to strengthen the economy amid a weakening global growth outlook. The domestic economy, however, remained resilient, expanding 5.1% year-on-year (y-o-y) in the second quarter (Q2) of 2025, up from 4.9% y-o-y in the prior quarter, with all major expenditure categories posting growth except for government spending. Consumer price inflation has ticked down to 2.3% y-o-y in August from 2.4% y-o-y in July and remained well within the target range of 1.5%–3.5%.

Figure 1: Indonesia's Benchmark Yield Curve—Local Currency Government Bonds

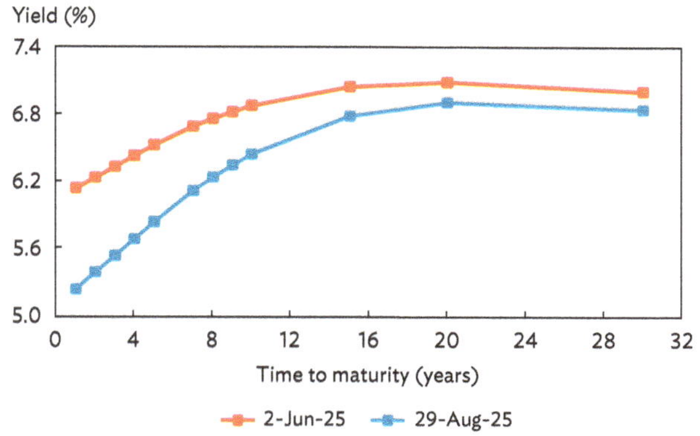

Source: Based on data from Bloomberg LP.

Figure 2: Composition of Local Currency Bonds Outstanding in Indonesia

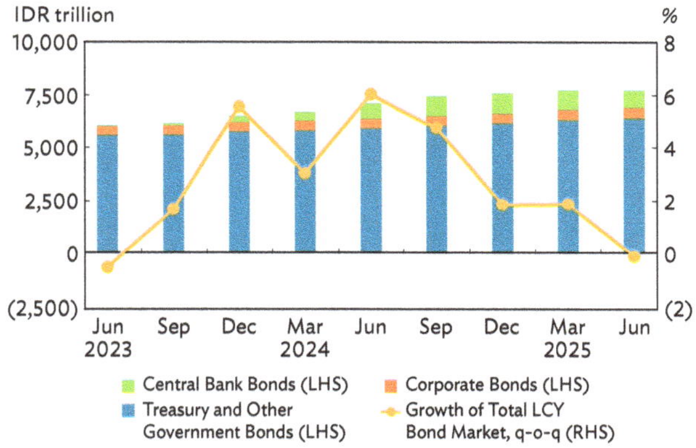

( ) = negative, IDR = Indonesian rupiah, LCY = local currency, LHS = left-hand side, q-o-q = quarter-on-quarter, RHS = right-hand side.

Sources: Bank Indonesia; Directorate General of Budget Financing and Risk Management, Ministry of Finance; and Indonesia Stock Exchange.

Local Currency Bond Market Size and Issuance

Outstanding LCY bonds in Indonesia recorded only a marginal decline in Q2 2025, dragged down by a contraction in the stock of central bank securities. Total LCY bonds outstanding size tallied IDR7,830.4 trillion at the end of June, posting a 0.1% quarter-on-quarter (q-o-q) contraction (**Figure 2**). Nonetheless, government bonds gained 1.3% q-o-q, albeit moderating from the previous quarter's 2.7% q-o-q expansion due to a large volume of maturities. Despite a slowdown in issuance, corporate bonds expanded 3.4% q-o-q in Q2 2025 over a reduced volume of maturities. Central bank securities extended their contraction, falling 11.3% q-o-q in Q2 2025, following a 3.4% q-o-q decline in the prior quarter, as maturities outpaced issuance as the central bank sought to expand the monetary base.

LCY bond issuance totaled IDR633.9 trillion in Q2 2025, down by a marginal 0.7% q-o-q, on reduced issuance in both the government and corporate bond segments. The government raised IDR259.2 trillion via Treasury instruments in Q2 2025, reflecting a slight dip in issuance growth of 0.4% q-o-q, due to a high base as the government continued its front-loading strategy (**Figure 3**). While the government is expected to post a wider budget deficit in 2025, excess savings from the 2024 budget will be utilized so that it will not be solely financed through debt issuance. Corporate bond issuance slipped 9.1% q-o-q in Q2 2025 amid caution over tariff uncertainties. The largest corporate bond issuances in Q2 2025 were from state-owned firms Perum Pegadaian,

This market summary was written by Roselyn Regalado, consultant, Economic Research and Development Impact Department, Asian Development Bank, Manila.

Figure 3: Composition of Local Currency Bond Issuance in Indonesia

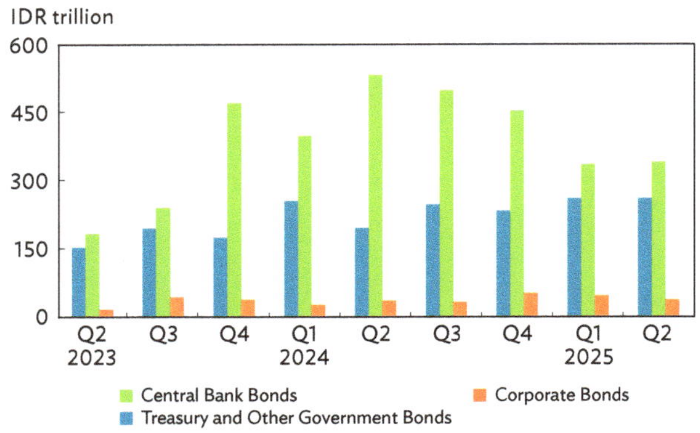

IDR = Indonesian rupiah, Q1 = first quarter, Q2 = second quarter, Q3 = third quarter, Q4 = fourth quarter.

Sources: Bank Indonesia; Directorate General of Budget Financing and Risk Management, Ministry of Finance; and Indonesia Stock Exchange.

Figure 4: Investor Profile of Tradable Government Bonds

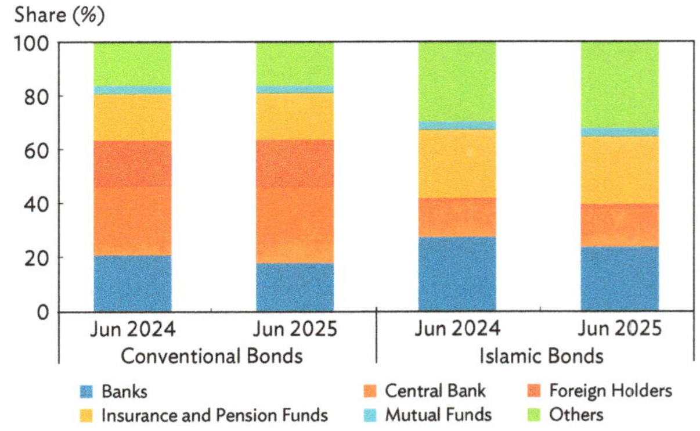

Source: Directorate General of Budget Financing and Risk Management, Ministry of Finance.

Bank Rakyat Indonesia, and Syariah Bank Indonesia, which together accounted for nearly half of the issuance total for the quarter.

Investor Profile

The central bank continued to account for the largest holdings of Treasury bonds at the end of June, equivalent to about a quarter of the total. Bank Indonesia's holdings of tradable government bonds ticked up from 23.1% a year earlier to 25.2% at the end of June as it continued to purchase Treasury bills and Treasury bonds to support its monetary operations.[22] Central bank holdings accounted for about 28.0% of conventional bonds and 14.0% of *sukuk* (Islamic bonds) (**Figure 4**). Banking institutions and insurance and pension funds were the next largest holders of Treasury bonds, with each accounting for a 19.0% share. Meanwhile, foreign investor holdings inched up to a 14.6% share of the total from 13.9% a year earlier, buoyed by investor bets on further policy rate cuts.

Sustainable Bond Market

At the end of June, Indonesia's sustainable bond market largely comprised green bonds and public sector issuance, with most bonds denominated in a foreign currency. Outstanding sustainable bonds totaled USD14.1 billion at the end of June, posting a contraction of 3.7% q-o-q in Q2 2025 following 2.7% q-o-q growth in the previous quarter. Green bonds continued to be the predominant bond type, accounting for 70.2% of the sustainable bond stock (**Figure 5**). Public sector entities were active issuers of green bonds (64.9% of the green bond stock) and sustainability bonds (80.8%), while the private sector dominated social bonds (98.7%) and sustainability-linked bonds (100.0%). Bonds with remaining tenors of over 5 years accounted for 58.9% of total sustainable bonds outstanding, largely driven by a higher share of longer-tenor maturities in government bonds (73.5%). This resulted in a size-weighted average tenor of 7.9 years. Foreign currency sustainable bonds outstanding comprised 62.5% of the entire bond stock at the end of June, with bonds denominated in United States dollars accounting for about half of the total.

Figure 5: Market Profile of Outstanding Sustainable Bonds in Indonesia at the End of June 2025

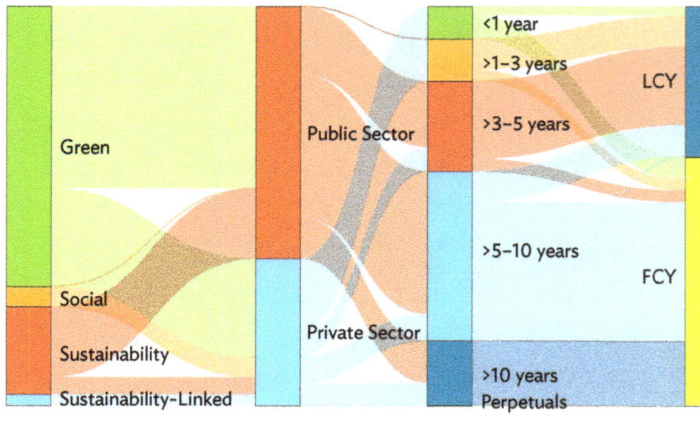

FCY = foreign currency, LCY = local currency.

Source: *AsianBondsOnline* calculations based on Bloomberg LP data.

[22] From 1 January to 19 August 2025, Bank Indonesia purchased IDR137.8 trillion of Treasury bonds from the secondary market and IDR48.3 trillion of Treasury bills from the primary market.

Republic of Korea

Yield Movements

Local currency (LCY) government bond yields in the Republic of Korea rose for most maturities between 2 June and 29 August on changing expectations of when the Bank of Korea (BOK) would resume monetary policy easing. Yields rose an average of 6 basis points (bps) for maturities of 1 year and longer, while declining an average of 2 bps for maturities of less than 1 year (**Figure 1**). The BOK left the base rate unchanged at 2.50% at its 10 July and 28 August meetings, following a 25 bps rate cut in May, amid uncertainty in the domestic economic growth outlook and as it continues to monitor developments in household debt and housing prices. The BOK in its August meeting noted that while economic growth has improved, risks to the outlook remain due to the United States' tariff policies. The BOK also raised its 2025 growth and inflation forecasts to 0.9% year-on-year (y-o-y) and 2.0% y-o-y, respectively, from the May forecasts of 0.8% y-o-y and 1.9% y-o-y. The Republic of Korea's economic growth inched up to 0.6% y-o-y in the second quarter (Q2) of 2025 after remaining unchanged in the previous quarter, driven by improved domestic consumption and continued export growth. Moreover, the increased bond supply due to the passing of the second supplementary budget in July also contributed to the rise in yields.

Figure 1: The Republic of Korea's Benchmark Yield Curve—Local Currency Government Bonds

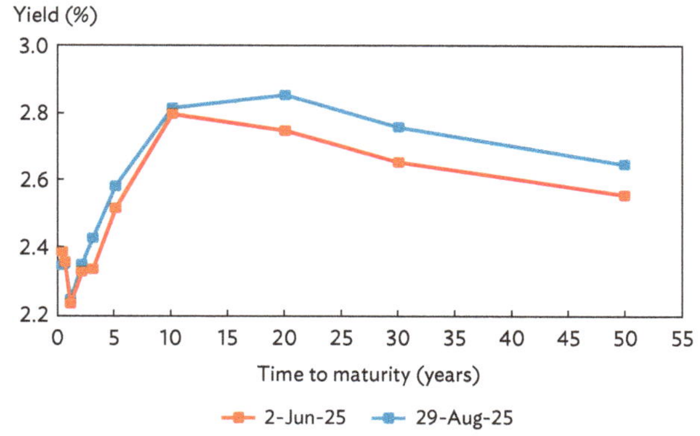

Source: Based on data from Bloomberg LP.

Local Currency Bond Market Size and Issuance

The Republic of Korea's LCY bonds outstanding grew 1.4% quarter-on-quarter (q-o-q) to KRW3,370.4 trillion at the end of June. Growth in Q2 2025 was higher than the 0.8% q-o-q marginal increase recorded in the first quarter (Q1) of 2025, supported by higher growth in both the government and corporate bond segments. Corporate bonds continued to dominate the bond market with a 57.6% share of total bonds outstanding at the end of June (**Figure 2**). Corporate bonds outstanding increased 0.3% q-o-q in Q2 2025, following a 0.1% q-o-q contraction in Q1 2025, due to a rebound in issuance. Meanwhile, government bonds rose 3.5% q-o-q in Q2 2025, driven by higher issuance during the quarter.

Figure 2: Composition of Local Currency Bonds Outstanding in the Republic of Korea

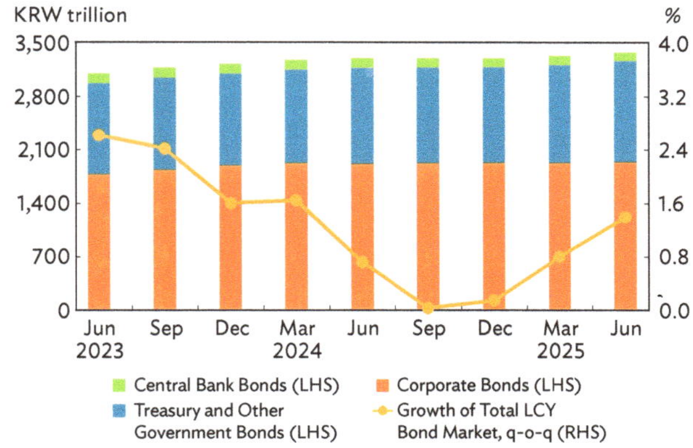

KRW = Korean won, LCY = local currency, LHS = left-hand side, q-o-q = quarter-on-quarter, RHS = right-hand side.
Sources: Bank of Korea and KG Zeroin Corp.

LCY bond issuance rebounded in Q2 2025 amid the government's expansionary fiscal policy and monetary policy easing. Total LCY bond issuance rose 11.3% q-o-q to KRW277.6 trillion in Q2 2025, led by higher issuance in both government and corporate segments (**Figure 3**). Government bond issuance increased 10.2% q-o-q in line with the government's front-loading policy in the first half of the year and also to fund the first supplementary budget approved in May. Corporate bond sales in the Republic of Korea rose 16.0% q-o-q in Q2 2025, a reversal

This market summary was written by Angelica Andrea Cruz, consultant, Economic Research and Development Impact Department, Asian Development Bank, Manila.

Figure 3: Composition of Local Currency Bond Issuance in the Republic of Korea

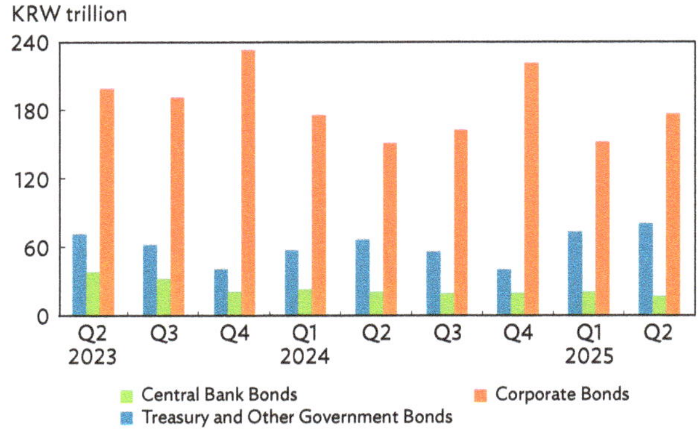

KRW = Korean won, Q1 = first quarter, Q2 = second quarter, Q3 = third quarter, Q4 = fourth quarter.
Sources: Bank of Korea and KG Zeroin Corp.

from the 31.0% q-o-q contraction in Q1 2025, as local firms front-loaded their bond issuance ahead of potential market volatility resulting from the June election. The expected policy rate cut by the BOK in May also provided a more favorable environment for bond issuance.

Investor Profile

Financial institutions continued to be the largest investor group in the Republic of Korea's LCY bond market. Insurance companies and pension funds (31.1%), banks (19.4%), and other financial institutions (15.3%) collectively accounted for a majority share of the LCY government bond market at the end of March (**Figure 4**). Foreign investors held 19.7% of government bonds outstanding, which was roughly at par with their holdings share at the end of March 2024. In the LCY corporate bond market, other financial institutions, insurance companies, and pension funds were the largest investor groups, accounting for nearly three-quarters of the total market. Meanwhile, foreign holdings in the corporate bond market remained negligible.

Sustainable Bond Market

Social bonds and green bonds continued to dominate the Republic of Korea's sustainable bond market. The Republic of Korea's sustainable bond market grew by 1.0% q-o-q to reach a size of USD184.9 billion at the end of June, mainly comprising social bonds and green bonds (**Figure 5**). Issuers in both the private and public sectors were active with nearly equal outstanding shares of 51.4% and 48.6%, respectively. Social bonds, of which almost three-quarters came from the public sector, comprised a majority (54.9%) of the total sustainable bond market. Meanwhile, green bonds, which were mostly issued by the private sector, had a share of 28.1% at the end of June. The size-weighted average maturity of outstanding sustainable bonds was 3.0 years at the end of June, while nearly 60% were denominated in Korean won.

Figure 4: Local Currency Bonds Outstanding Investor Profile

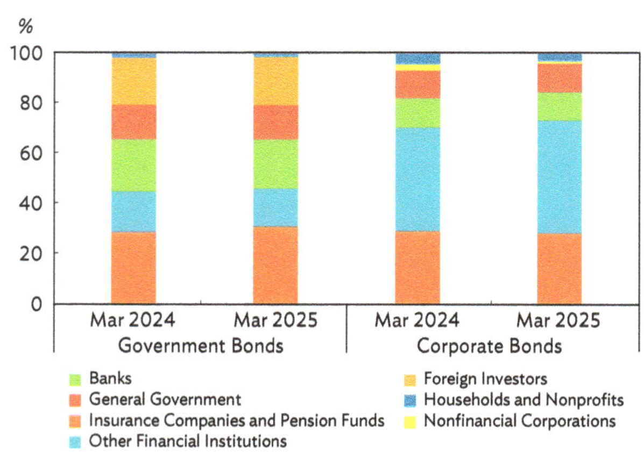

Sources: *AsianBondsOnline* and Bank of Korea.

Figure 5: Market Profile of Outstanding Sustainable Bonds in the Republic of Korea at the End of June 2025

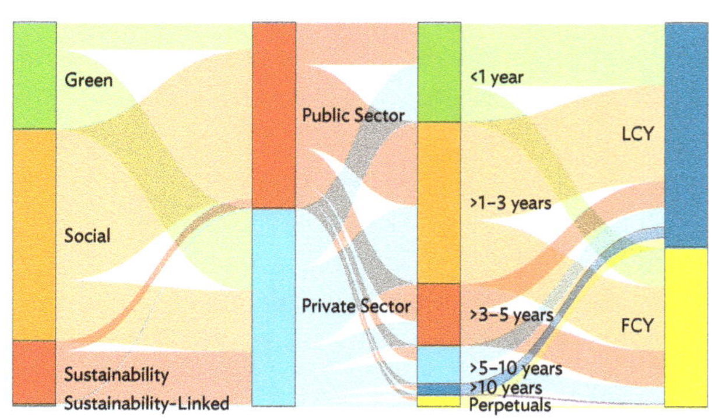

FCY = foreign currency, LCY = local currency.
Source: *AsianBondsOnline* calculations based on Bloomberg LP data.

Malaysia

Yield Movements

Malaysia's local currency (LCY) government bond yield curve shifted downward between 2 June and 29 August. Bond yields fell an average of 14 basis points across all maturities amid monetary policy easing by Bank Negara Malaysia (BNM) (**Figure 1**). On 9 July, the BNM reduced the overnight policy rate for the first time in 2 years to 2.75%, while on 4 September, it held the policy rate steady, as preemptive measures to keep Malaysia on a steady growth path. In the second quarter (Q2) of 2025, Malaysia's economy grew 4.4% year-on-year, the same pace as the previous quarter, and well within the government's target of 4.0%–4.8%. Q2 2025's growth was partly driven by sustained growth in exports along with an expansion in private consumption, which was supported by policy measures to increase household spending. The BNM and the Government of Malaysia also recognized external downside risks to growth resulting from weakening global trade and muted investor sentiment.

Figure 1: Malaysia's Benchmark Yield Curve—Local Currency Government Bonds

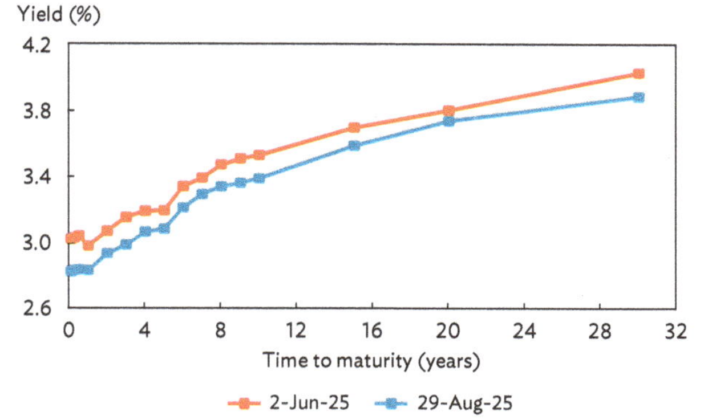

Source: Based on data from Bloomberg LP.

Local Currency Bond Market Size and Issuance

The LCY bond market of Malaysia expanded in Q2 2025, driven by growth in Treasury bonds. The LCY bond market reached a size of MYR2.2 trillion on growth of 1.9% quarter-on-quarter (q-o-q) in Q2 2025, following the first quarter's (Q1) 2.3% q-o-q expansion (**Figure 2**). Outstanding Treasuries and other government bonds rose 2.6% q-o-q, despite a contraction in issuance due to a lower volume of maturities during the quarter. Malaysia's corporate bond segment posted 1.1% q-o-q growth in Q2 2025, down from the previous quarter's 2.0% q-o-q growth on increased maturities. *Sukuk* (Islamic bonds) continued to comprise a majority of the LCY bond market with a share of 63.5% at the end of June.

Figure 2: Composition of Local Currency Bonds Outstanding in Malaysia

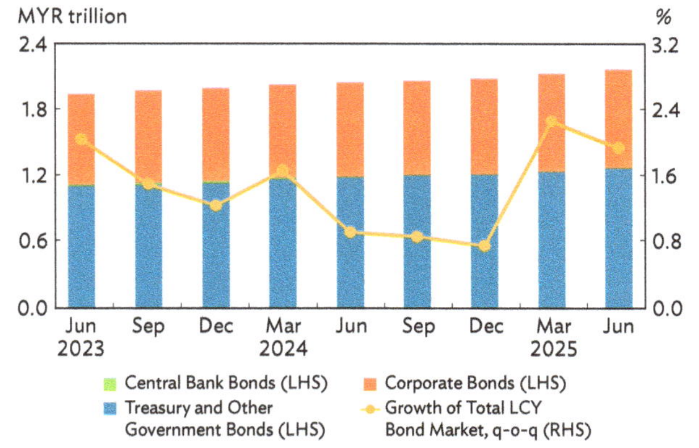

LCY = local currency, LHS = left-hand side, MYR = Malaysian ringgit, q-o-q = quarter-on-quarter, RHS = right-hand side.
Source: Bank Negara Malaysia Fully Automated System for Issuing/Tendering.

LCY bond issuance contracted 12.9% q-o-q in Q2 2025, a reversal of Q1 2025's 23.9% growth. Government bond issuance fell 22.3% q-o-q in Q2 2025, following a 63.5% q-o-q expansion in Q1 2025, as issuance was front-loaded in the first several months of the year (**Figure 3**). Corporate bond sales comprised over half (53.9%) of total issuance in Q2 2025 but saw a 2.7% q-o-q contraction, weighed down by trade uncertainties. Maybank Islamic led LCY corporate bond issuances in Q2 2025 with its debt sales of commercial paper *sukuk* and corporate *sukuk* totaling MYR5.5 billion, or 11.8% of total LCY corporate issuance.

This market summary was written by Justin Adrian Villas, consultant, Economic Research and Development Impact Department, Asian Development Bank, Manila.

Figure 3: Composition of Local Currency Bond Issuance in Malaysia

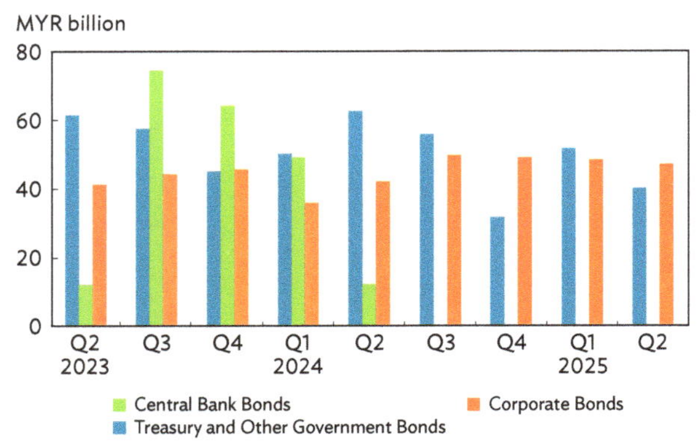

MYR = Malaysian ringgit, Q1 = first quarter, Q2 = second quarter, Q3 = third quarter, Q4 = fourth quarter.

Source: Bank Negara Malaysia Fully Automated System for Issuing/Tendering.

Investor Profile

At the end of March, domestic investors held 79.2% of Malaysia's LCY government bonds outstanding. Malaysia's LCY government bond market was dominated by financial institutions and social security institutions—together comprising an aggregate bond holdings share of 61.2% (**Figure 4**). The share of foreign holdings in Malaysia's government bond market fell to 20.8% at the end of March from 21.2% a year prior on increased uncertainty over the Federal Reserve's monetary policy outlook. Nevertheless, Malaysia maintained the highest foreign holdings share within emerging East Asia.[23]

Sustainable Bond Market

At the end of June, corporate bonds dominated Malaysia's sustainable bond market, which mainly comprised sustainability bonds and bonds denominated in Malaysian ringgit. Outstanding sustainable bonds in Malaysia expanded 2.0% q-o-q, tallying USD16.0 billion at the end of June, 68.9% of which were sustainability bonds, followed by green bonds at 19.0% (**Figure 5**). At the end of June, 78.1% of outstanding sustainable bonds had been issued by corporates, with over half (58.9%) of corporate issuances carrying tenors longer than 5 years. On the other hand, bonds issued by the public sector, which made up 21.9% of total outstanding sustainable bonds, all carried tenors of over 5 years. This resulted in a size-weighted average tenor of 8.3 years in Malaysia's sustainable bond market. A large majority (88.5%) of total sustainable bonds outstanding were denominated in Malaysian ringgit.

Figure 4: Local Currency Government Bonds Investor Profile

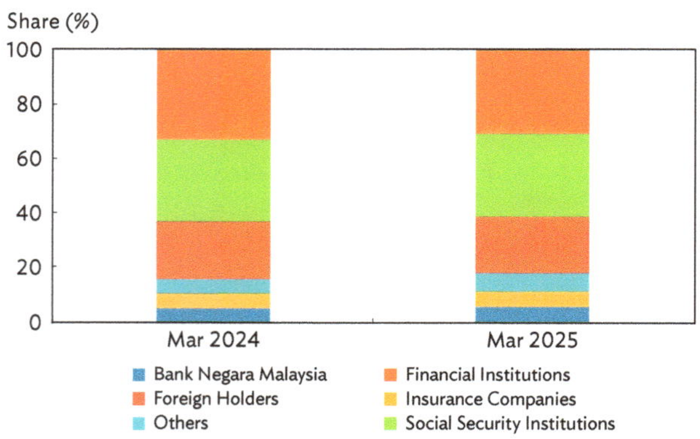

Note: "Others" include statutory bodies, nominees and trustee companies, and cooperatives and unclassified items.

Source: Bank Negara Malaysia.

Figure 5: Market Profile of Outstanding Sustainable Bonds in Malaysia at the End of June 2025

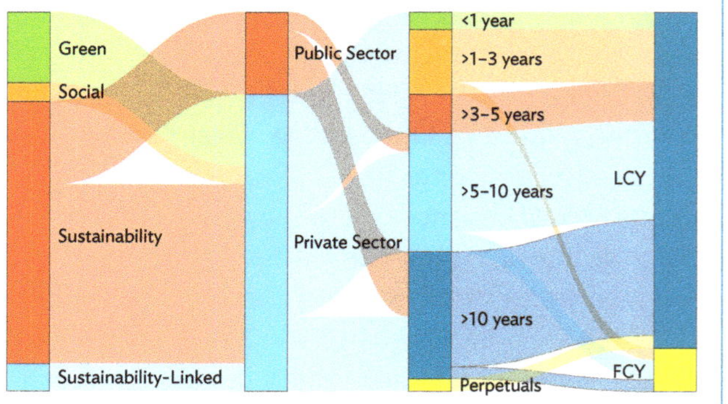

FCY = foreign currency, LCY = local currency.

Source: *AsianBondsOnline* calculations based on Bloomberg LP data.

[23] Emerging East Asia is defined to include member states of the Association of Southeast Asian Nations plus the People's Republic of China; Hong Kong, China; and the Republic of Korea.

Philippines

Yield Movements

Between 2 June and 29 August, the local currency (LCY) sovereign bond yield curve in the Philippines shifted downward across all maturities. Yields across the curve fell an average of 17 basis points on a dovish monetary policy stance by the Bangko Sentral ng Pilipinas (BSP) amid easing inflation and a slowing economy (**Figure 1**). On 19 June and 28 August, the BSP reduced its policy rate by 25 basis points each, lowering the overnight reverse repurchase rate to 5.00%. Inflation remained subdued despite accelerating to 1.5% year-on-year (y-o-y) in August from 0.9% y-o-y in July, staying below the target range of 2.0%–3.0%. On 26 June, the government lowered its 2025 growth target to a range of 5.5%–6.5% from the previous target of 6.0%–8.0% set in December 2024, citing heightened growth risks stemming from external policy uncertainty and Middle East tensions. In the second quarter (Q2) of 2025, the Philippine economy grew 5.5% y-o-y, up from 5.4% y-o-y in the previous quarter, driven by resilient household consumption (5.5% y-o-y). On 11 August, the BSP signaled two more rate cuts in 2025 to foster economic growth.

Figure 1: The Philippines' Benchmark Yield Curve—Local Currency Government Bonds

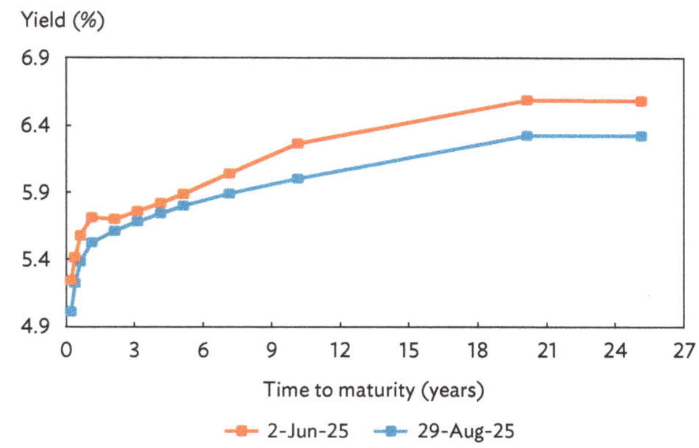

Source: Based on data from Bloomberg LP.

Figure 2: Composition of Local Currency Bonds Outstanding in the Philippines

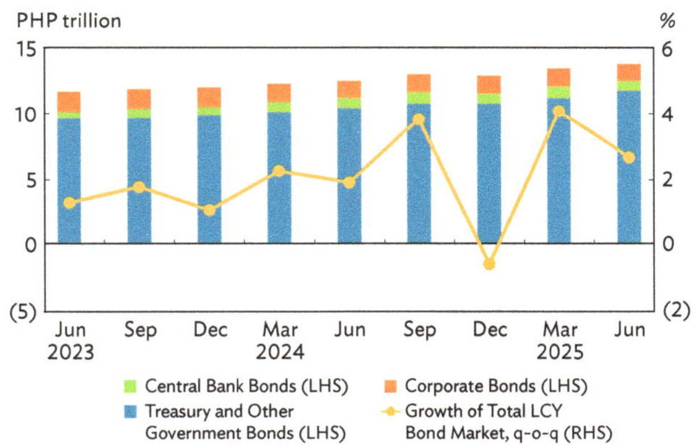

( ) = negative, LCY = local currency, LHS = left-hand side, PHP = Philippine peso, q-o-q = quarter-on-quarter, RHS = right-hand side.

Note: Treasury and other government bonds comprise Treasury bonds, Treasury bills, and bonds issued by government agencies, entities, and corporations for which repayment is guaranteed by the Government of the Philippines.

Sources: Bangko Sentral ng Pilipinas, Bureau of the Treasury, and Bloomberg LP.

Local Currency Bond Market Size and Issuance

Contractions in central bank securities and corporate bonds outstanding weighed on LCY bond market growth in Q2 2025. At the end of June, outstanding LCY bonds reached PHP13.8 trillion on growth of 2.7% quarter-on-quarter (q-o-q), slower than the 4.1% q-o-q expansion in the previous quarter (**Figure 2**). The moderated growth was driven by contractions in the stock of central bank securities (–18.9% q-o-q) and corporate bonds (–4.0% q-o-q) due to reduced issuances during the quarter. Meanwhile, growth in outstanding Treasury and other government bonds accelerated to 5.2% q-o-q in Q2 2025 on increased issuance from the government amid a favorable interest rate environment.

LCY bond issuance slowed in Q2 2025 amid global trade uncertainty. During the quarter, total LCY bond issuance tallied PHP2.7 trillion on marginal growth of 0.5% q-o-q (**Figure 3**). Corporate bond issuance declined 23.5% q-o-q in Q2 2025, as companies delayed expansion plans amid uncertainty surrounding trade. The Bank of the Philippine Islands issued the largest corporate bond via the sale of its Supporting Inclusion, Nature, and Growth Bonds worth PHP40.0 billion, accounting for 71.4% of the corporate issuance total. Issuance of central bank securities also declined (–13.2% q-o-q) during the quarter as the BSP aimed to support financial market activity. In contrast, Treasury

This market summary was written by Jeremy Grace Ilustrisimo, consultant, Economic Research and Development Impact Department, Asian Development Bank, Manila.

Figure 3: Composition of Local Currency Bond Issuance in the Philippines

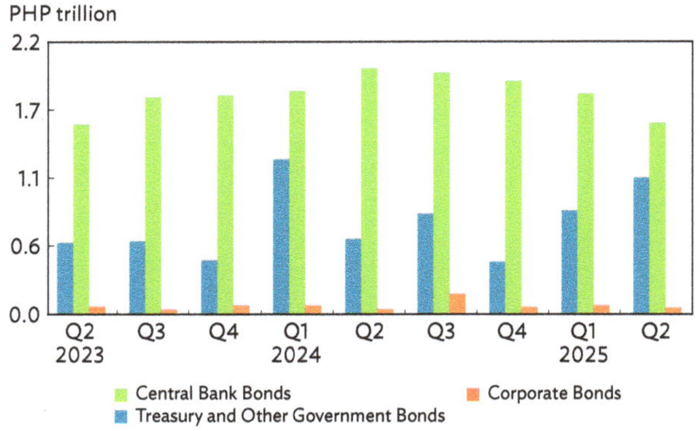

PHP = Philippine peso, Q1 = first quarter, Q2 = second quarter, Q3 = third quarter, Q4 = fourth quarter.

Note: Treasury and other government bonds comprise Treasury bonds, Treasury bills, and bonds issued by government agencies, entities, and corporations for which repayment is guaranteed by the Government of the Philippines.

Sources: Bangko Sentral ng Pilipinas, Bureau of the Treasury, and Bloomberg LP.

Figure 4: Investor Profile of Local Currency Government Bonds

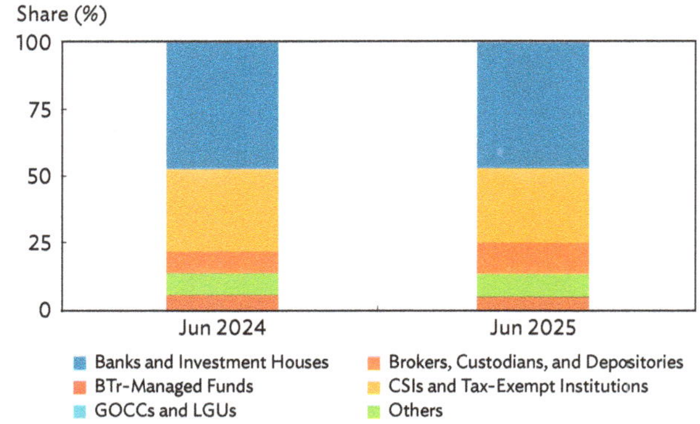

BTr = Bureau of the Treasury, CSI = contractual savings institution, GOCC = government-owned or -controlled corporation, LGU = local government unit.

Note: At the end of June 2025, the aggregate holdings share for GOCCs and LGUs was 0.003%, amounting to PHP0.3 billion.

Source: Bureau of the Treasury.

and other government bond issuance rose 32.0% q-o-q in Q2 2025, buoyed by the government's issuance of 10-year benchmark bonds worth PHP300.0 billion in April.

Investor Profile

Banks and investment houses remained the largest holding group of government securities at the end of June. This investor group held 46.5% of the government's total debt stock at the end of June, slightly down from 46.9% a year earlier (**Figure 4**). This was followed by contractual savings institutions and tax-exempt institutions, whose respective bond holdings declined to 28.1% from 30.9% during the same period. Among all investor groups, brokers, custodians, and depositories posted the largest increase in bond holdings during the review period, rising to 11.5% at the end of June from 8.1% the previous year, making it the third-largest investor group in the LCY government bond market.

Sustainable Bond Market

The Philippines' sustainable bond market mainly comprises sustainability instruments financed by both the public and private sectors. Sustainability bonds accounted for 87.2% of the market's total sustainable debt stock in Q2 2025, about 60% and 40% of which were issued by the public and private sectors, respectively (**Figure 5**). At the end of June, total outstanding sustainable bonds grew 5.3% q-o-q to USD14.3 billion, accounting for only 2.0% of emerging East Asia's total sustainable debt stock in Q2 2025.[24] Outstanding sustainable bonds were largely concentrated in tenors of over 10 years (46.4%), which brought the market's size-weighted average tenor to 11.8 years at the end of June. The United States dollar was the predominant issuance currency among outstanding sustainable bonds with a share of 57.6%. This was followed by the Philippine peso (31.4%), euro (7.2%), and Japanese yen (3.8%).

Figure 5: Market Profile of Outstanding Sustainable Bonds in the Philippines at the End of June 2025

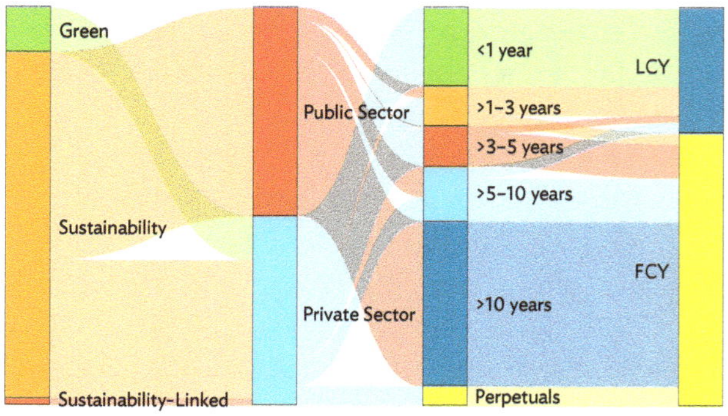

FCY = foreign currency, LCY = local currency.

Source: *AsianBondsOnline* calculations based on Bloomberg LP data.

[24] Emerging East Asia is defined to include member states of the Association of Southeast Asian Nations plus the People's Republic of China; Hong Kong, China; and the Republic of Korea.

Singapore

Yield Movements

Between 2 June and 29 August, the local currency (LCY) government bond yield curve in Singapore shifted downward. Bond yields fell an average of 61 basis points across the curve amid cooling inflation and expectations of slower economic growth (**Figure 1**). On 30 July, the Monetary Authority of Singapore (MAS) maintained its monetary policy stance on better-than-expected growth momentum and subdued inflationary pressures. In the second quarter (Q2) of 2025, the economy grew 4.4% year-on-year (y-o-y), higher than the initial estimate of 4.3% y-o-y, partly driven by rapid growth in the wholesale trade and manufacturing industries. However, the q-o-q growth forecast for the third and fourth quarters of the year is only 1.5%–2.5%. In July, consumer price inflation was 0.6% y-o-y, ticking downward from 0.8% y-o-y in both May and June, but still within the inflation forecast of 0.5%–1.5% y-o-y.

Figure 1: Singapore's Benchmark Yield Curve—Local Currency Government Bonds

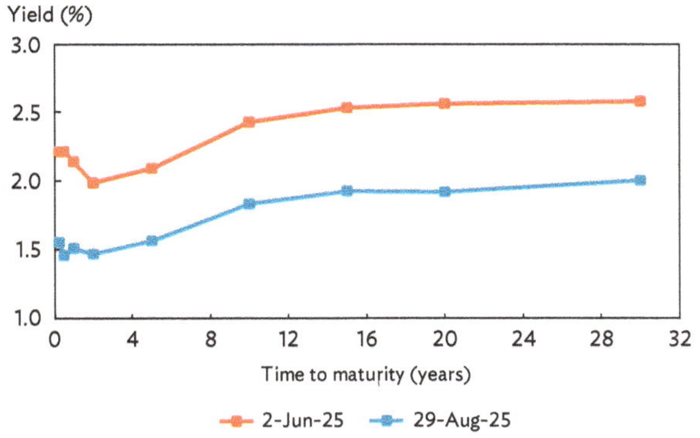

Source: Based on data from Bloomberg LP.

Local Currency Bond Market Size and Issuance

Singapore's LCY bond market increased to a size of SGD872.1 billion at the end of June, driven by growth in outstanding MAS bills. The LCY bond market inched up 0.6% quarter-on-quarter (q-o-q) in Q2 2025, extending the growth of 2.0% q-o-q in the first quarter (Q1) (**Figure 2**). The stock of outstanding MAS bills rose 1.9% q-o-q, up from 1.5% q-o-q growth in Q1 2025. Meanwhile, Treasuries and other government bonds saw subdued expansion, only gaining 0.7% q-o-q in Q2 2025, compared to 3.5% q-o-q in the prior quarter due to a high volume of maturities. Corporate bonds outstanding contracted 1.8% q-o-q, a reversal from the 0.7% q-o-q growth in Q1 2025, on reduced corporate issuance.

Figure 2: Composition of Local Currency Bonds Outstanding in Singapore

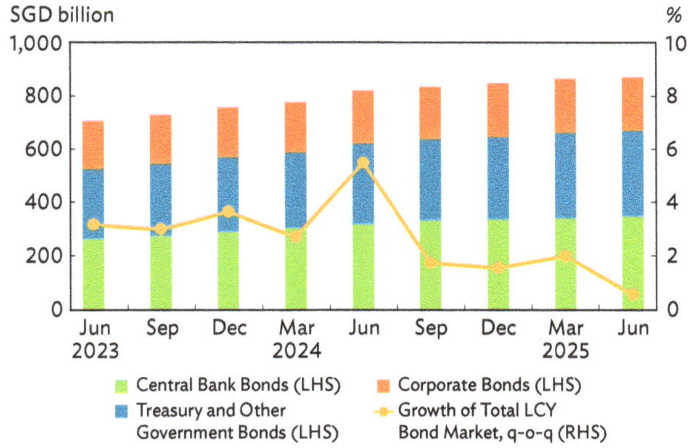

LCY = local currency, LHS = left-hand side, q-o-q = quarter-on-quarter, RHS = right-hand side, SGD = Singapore dollar.

Note: Corporate bonds are based on *AsianBondsOnline* estimates.

Sources: Monetary Authority of Singapore and Bloomberg LP.

This market summary was written by Justin Adrian Villas, consultant, Economic Research and Development Impact Department, Asian Development Bank, Manila.

Total LCY bond issuance inched up in Q2 2025, buoyed by growth in Treasury and other government bonds. Bond market sales totaled SGD573.2 billion in Q2 2025 on 1.4% q-o-q growth, faster than the previous quarter's pace of 0.7% q-o-q (**Figure 3**). Issuance of Treasury and other government bonds grew the fastest at 19.9% q-o-q in Q2 2025, compared to Q1 2025's 0.2% q-o-q. On the other hand, issuance of MAS bills only marginally increased 0.1% q-o-q. The corporate bond segment saw a large contraction of 70.6% q-o-q partly due to trade market uncertainties dampening corporate plans for expansion. CapitaLand led corporate bond issuance in Q2 2025, issuing perpetual securities worth SGD260.0 million, or 19.3% of total corporate issuance, as part of its debt issuance program.

Figure 3: Composition of Local Currency Bond Issuance in Singapore

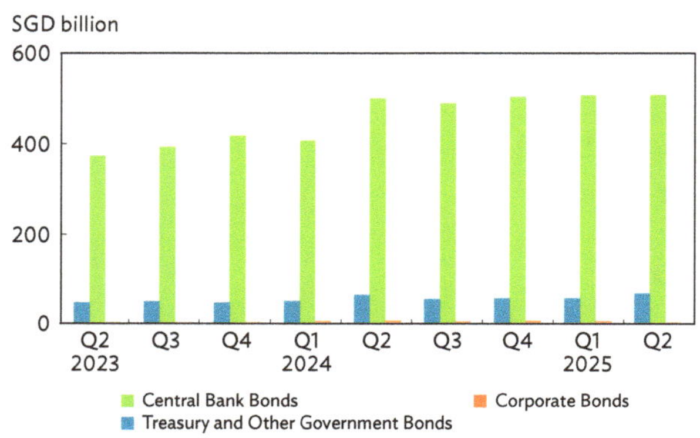

Q1 = first quarter, Q2 = second quarter, Q3 = third quarter, Q4 = fourth quarter, SGD = Singapore dollar.

Notes:

1. Corporate bonds are based on *AsianBondsOnline* estimates.
2. Corporate bond issuance on Q2 2025 totaled SGD1.3 billion.

Sources: Monetary Authority of Singapore and Bloomberg LP.

Sustainable Bond Market

Singapore's sustainable bond market is dominated by green bond instruments, which accounted for 84.6% of total outstanding sustainable bonds at the end of June. The sustainable bond stock rose to USD28.0 billion at the end of Q2 2025 on growth of 5.4% q-o-q, up from a 2.3% q-o-q increase recorded in Q1 2025 (**Figure 4**). A majority (83.3%) of outstanding sustainable bonds were denominated in Singapore dollars. Bonds with tenors of more than 5 years comprised 59.7% of the total sustainable bond stock at the end of Q2 2025. The largest issuer of sustainable bonds during the quarter was the Government of Singapore as it issued a 29-year bond worth SGD1.8 billion to support green public sector projects. As a result, the size-weighted average tenor was 16.6 years, the longest among its emerging East Asian peers.[25]

Figure 4: Market Profile of Outstanding Sustainable Bonds in Singapore at the End of June 2025

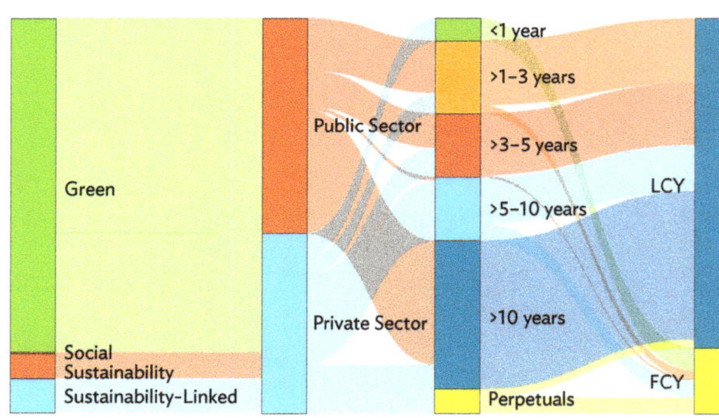

FCY = foreign currency, LCY = local currency.

Source: *AsianBondsOnline* calculations based on Bloomberg LP data.

[25] Emerging East Asia is defined to include member states of the Association of Southeast Asian Nations plus the People's Republic of China; Hong Kong, China; and the Republic of Korea.

Thailand

Yield Movements

Between 2 June and 29 August, Thailand's local currency (LCY) government bond yield curve shifted downward in response to monetary policy easing by the Bank of Thailand (BOT). Yields fell by an average of 46 basis points across the curve following the central bank's policy rate cut on 13 August (**Figure 1**). The central bank lowered its policy rate by 25 basis points each during its February, April, and August monetary policy meetings to support the economy amid trade uncertainty and subdued inflation. Gross domestic product growth slowed to 2.8% year-on-year (y-o-y) in the second quarter (Q2) of 2025 from 3.2% y-o-y in the first quarter (Q1), mainly due to a weaker expansion in nonagricultural production, particularly tourism-related activities. The BOT expects economic growth to decelerate further in the second half of 2025 given downside risks from United States tariffs and slowing global growth. Consumer price inflation had been in negative territory since April and declined further to −0.8% y-o-y in August from −0.7% y-o-y in July and −0.3% y-o-y in June due to lower energy and food prices.

Figure 1: Thailand's Benchmark Yield Curve—Local Currency Government Bonds

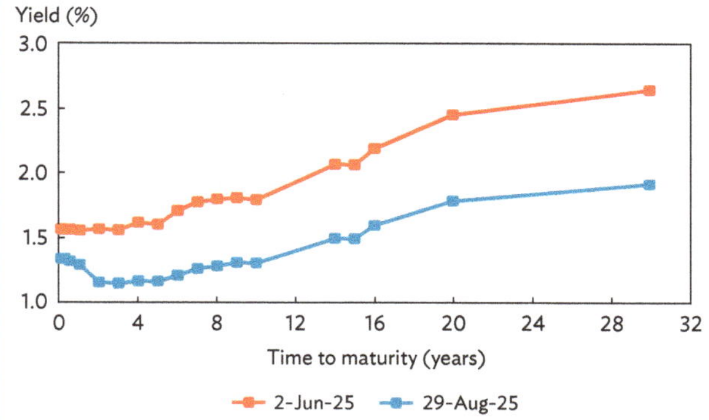

Sources: Based on data from Bloomberg LP and Thai Bond Market Association.

Figure 2: Composition of Local Currency Bonds Outstanding in Thailand

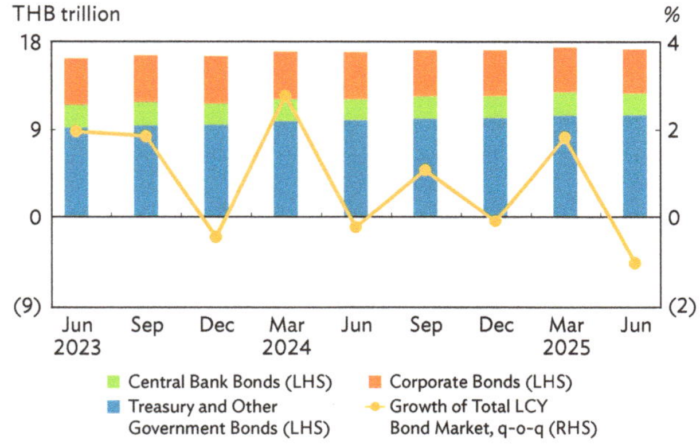

( ) = negative, LCY = local currency, LHS = left-hand side, q-o-q = quarter-on-quarter, RHS = right-hand side, THB = Thai baht.

Sources: Bank of Thailand and Thai Bond Market Association.

Local Currency Bond Market Size and Issuance

Thailand's LCY bond market contracted in Q2 2025 on a weakening expansion in government bonds and a decline in corporate bonds. Outstanding LCY bonds amounted to THB17.2 trillion at the end of June, down 1.0% quarter-on-quarter (q-o-q) in Q2 2025 compared to a 1.8% q-o-q rise in the previous quarter (**Figure 2**). Government bonds posted slower growth and corporate bonds continued to contract in Q2 2025. The expansion in government bonds decelerated to 0.4% q-o-q in Q2 2025 from 2.6% q-o-q in the prior quarter, owing to a larger volume of maturities. Meanwhile, corporate bonds continued to contract at a pace of −2.0% q-o-q in Q2 2025 as maturities outpaced issuance. Treasury and other government bonds (THB10.4 trillion) comprised 60.6% of the LCY bond market at the end of June, while corporate bonds (THB4.4 trillion) and BOT bonds (THB2.3 trillion) accounted for the remaining 25.8% and 13.6% shares, respectively.

Issuance of LCY bonds rose 2.2% q-o-q to THB2.2 trillion in Q2 2025, driven by increased issuance of government bonds. LCY bond issuance growth in Q2 2025 was broadly comparable to the 2.4% q-o-q gain in the previous quarter (**Figure 3**). Government bond issuance rose 2.0% q-o-q in Q2 2025, up from 0.2% q-o-q in Q1 2025, on increased government borrowing to finance stimulus measures. In June, Thailand's cabinet approved an economic stimulus

This market summary was written by Debbie Gundaya, consultant, Economic Research and Development Impact Department, Asian Development Bank, Manila.

Figure 3: Composition of Local Currency Bond Issuance in Thailand

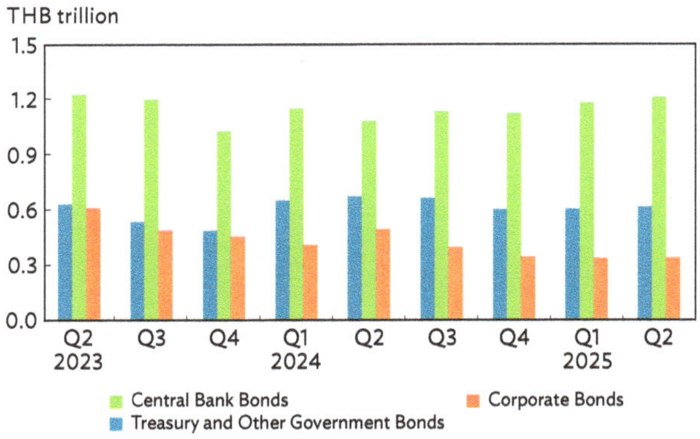

Q1 = first quarter, Q2 = second quarter, Q3 = third quarter, Q4 = fourth quarter, THB = Thai baht.

Sources: Bank of Thailand and Thai Bond Market Association.

package worth THB151.0 billion intended to support infrastructure projects and tourism. Meanwhile, corporate bond sales recovered slightly in Q2 2025, edging up 0.8% q-o-q after 3 consecutive quarters of contraction as firms took advantage of a low-interest-rate environment amid monetary policy easing by the BOT. SCBX, a bank, was the largest corporate issuer in Q2 2025 with total debt sales of THB20.0 billion, accounting for 5.9% of total corporate bond issuance during the quarter.

Investor Profile

Insurance and pension funds remained the largest holding group of Thai Treasury bonds at the end of June. Nonetheless, insurance and pension funds' holdings share inched down to 43.0% at the end of June from 43.6% a year earlier (**Figure 4**). Meanwhile, banks' holdings share edged up to 22.3% from 21.4% during the same period. These two investor groups remained the top holders of Thai Treasury bonds.

Figure 4: Investor Profile of Government Bonds in Thailand

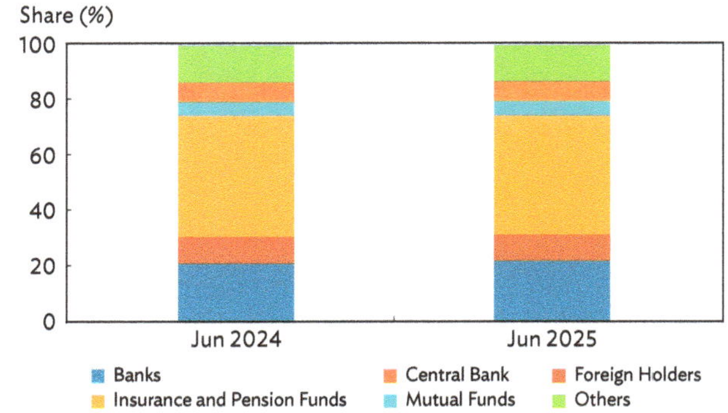

Source: Bank of Thailand.

Sustainable Bond Market

Thailand's sustainable bonds outstanding reached USD26.4 billion at the end of June and remained dominated by public sector sustainability bonds. The Thai sustainable bond market continued to post robust growth, expanding 4.8% q-o-q in Q2 2025 after a 4.6% q-o-q increase in Q1 2025. Sustainability instruments continued to comprise the largest share at 60.8% of the total (**Figure 4**). Following large issuances from both the public and private sectors in Q2 2025, sustainability-linked instruments were the second-most predominant bond type at the end of June with an 18.6% share. The market share of green bonds outstanding edged down to 16.2% at the end of June from 17.6% at the end of March. Nearly 70% of outstanding sustainable bonds were issued by the public sector, and these were predominantly sustainability instruments with longer tenors. About 64.1% of outstanding sustainable bonds had remaining tenors longer than 10 years, resulting in a size-weighted average tenor of 9.0 years at the end of June. LCY-denominated bonds accounted for 98.5% of sustainable bonds in Thailand, which remained among the highest shares in emerging East Asia.[26]

Figure 5: Market Profile of Outstanding Sustainable Bonds in Thailand at the End of June 2025

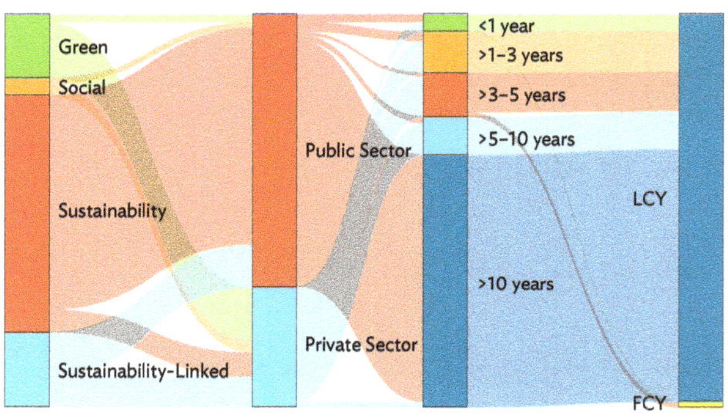

FCY = foreign currency, LCY = local currency.

Source: *AsianBondsOnline* calculations based on Bloomberg LP data.

[26] Emerging East Asia is defined to include member states of the Association of Southeast Asian Nations plus the People's Republic of China; Hong Kong, China; and the Republic of Korea.

Viet Nam

Yield Movements

The local currency (LCY) sovereign bond yield curve in Viet Nam shifted upward across all maturities between 2 June and 29 August. Yields across the curve climbed an average of 49 basis points, propelled by strong economic growth and relatively high inflation (**Figure 1**). In the second quarter (Q2) of 2025, Viet Nam's economy grew the fastest among its emerging East Asian peers, expanding 8.0% year-on-year (y-o-y) compared with 6.9% y-o-y in the previous quarter.[27] The Q2 2025 growth surpassed the government's expectation (7.7% y-o-y) and was supported by expansions in the manufacturing and construction (9.0% y-o-y) and service (8.5% y-o-y) sectors. On 5 August, the government revised upward the 2025 growth target to a range of 8.3%–8.5% from a target of at least 8.0% set in February to boost economic momentum and lay a foundation for double-digit growth in 2026. Inflation eased to 3.2% y-o-y in both August and July from 3.6% y-o-y in June, driven by moderating food prices and declining transportation cost. Despite this decline, Viet Nam's August inflation was also the highest among its regional peers, but it remained within the government's ceiling of 4.5%.

Figure 1: Viet Nam's Benchmark Yield Curve—Local Currency Government Bonds

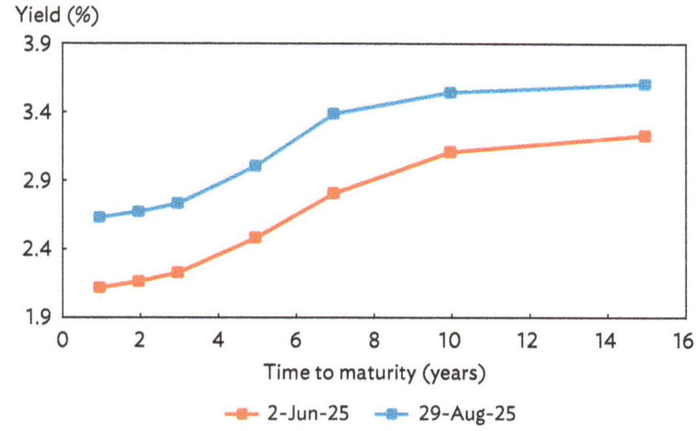

Source: Based on data from Bloomberg LP.

Local Currency Bond Market Size and Issuance

LCY bond market growth accelerated in Q2 2025, supported by expansions across all bond segments. At the end of June, the total LCY debt stock reached VND3,487.0 trillion on accelerated growth of 8.2% quarter-on-quarter (q-o-q) versus 1.9% q-o-q growth in the previous quarter (**Figure 2**). Outstanding corporate bonds grew 13.6% q-o-q in Q2 2025, driven by increased issuance from corporates and the growing participation of nonbank entities. Despite reduced issuance, outstanding Treasury and other government bonds and central bank securities recorded q-o-q growth of 3.5% and 77.2%, respectively, supported by fewer maturities during the quarter.

Figure 2: Composition of Local Currency Bonds Outstanding in Viet Nam

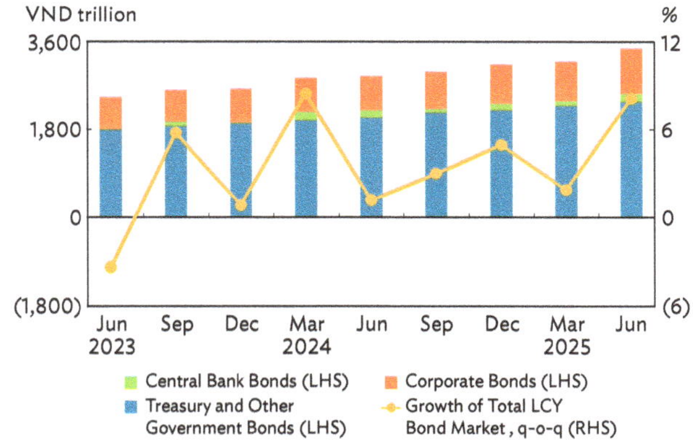

() = negative, LCY = local currency, LHS = left-hand side, q-o-q = quarter-on-quarter, RHS = right-hand side, VND = Vietnamese dong.

Note: Other government bonds comprise government-guaranteed and municipal bonds.

Sources: Hanoi Stock Exchange, State Bank of Vietnam, Vietnam Bond Market Association, and Bloomberg LP.

Reduced debt sales from both the government and central bank fueled the decline in total LCY bond issuance. In Q2 2025, overall issuance dropped 40.2% q-o-q to VND742.6 trillion, reversing the previous quarter's 33.0% q-o-q growth (**Figure 3**). Issuance of Treasury and other government bonds contracted 17.6% q-o-q due to investors preference for only the 5-year and 10-year instruments amid lingering global trade uncertainty. Central bank securities posted the fastest q-o-q decline in issuance at 56.6% as the

This market summary was written by Jeremy Grace Ilustrisimo, consultant, Economic Research and Development Impact Department, Asian Development Bank, Manila.

[27] Emerging East Asia is defined to include member states of the Association of Southeast Asian Nations plus the People's Republic of China; Hong Kong, China; and the Republic of Korea.

Figure 3: Composition of Local Currency Bond Issuance in Viet Nam

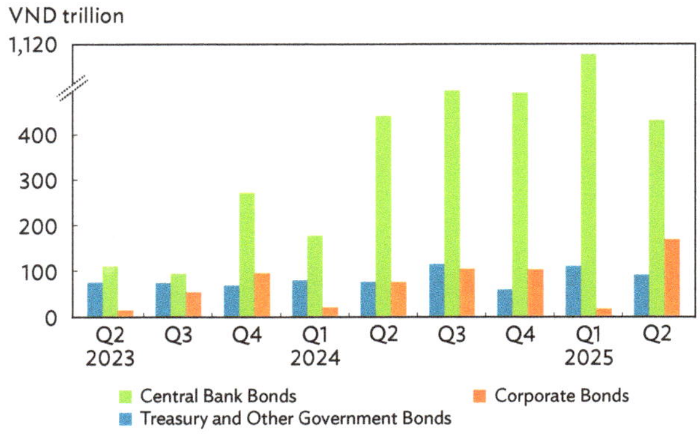

Q1 = first quarter, Q2 = second quarter, Q3 = third quarter, Q4 = fourth quarter, VND = Vietnamese dong.

Note: Other government bonds comprise government-guaranteed and municipal bonds.

Sources: Hanoi Stock Exchange, State Bank of Vietnam, Vietnam Bond Market Association, and Bloomberg LP.

Figure 4: Market Profile of the Two Dominant Investors for Local Currency Government Bonds

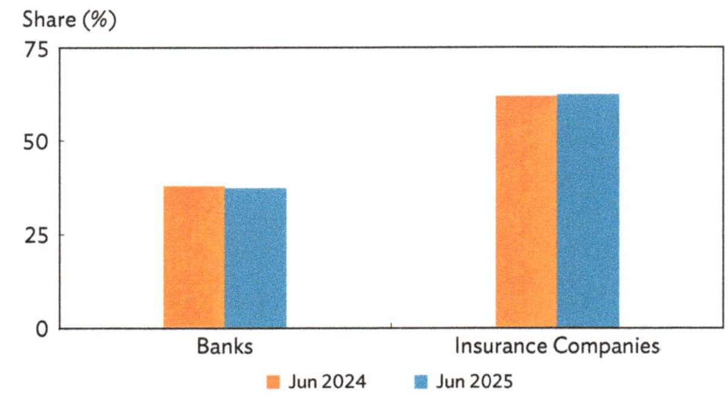

Source: Ministry of Finance, Viet Nam.

Figure 5: Market Profile of Outstanding Sustainable Bonds in Viet Nam at the End of June 2025

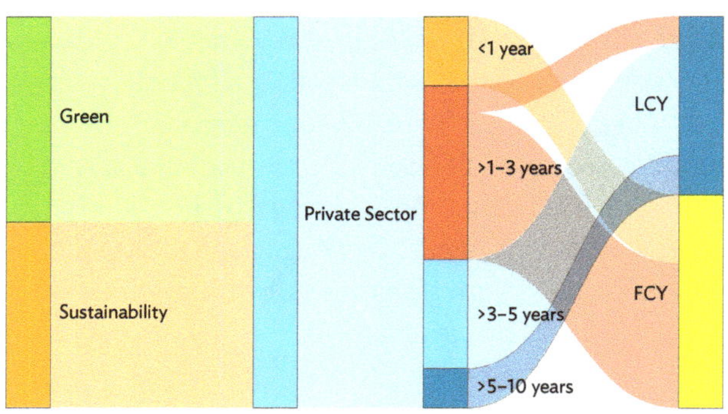

FCY = foreign currency, LCY = local currency.

Source: *AsianBondsOnline* calculations based on Bloomberg LP data.

State Bank of Vietnam aimed to stimulate financial market activity to meet the credit growth target of 16.0%. In contrast, corporate bond issuance grew more than tenfold in Q2 2025 to VND167.8 trillion, driven by banks' need to raise capital to meet the credit growth target set by the central bank and nonfinancial firms' need for refinancing as repayment pressure is expected to peak in the third quarter. The banking and property sectors were the key drivers of issuance during the quarter, accounting for 72.4% and 21.0%, respectively, of the corporate issuance total in Q2 2025.

Investor Profile

The investor profile of Viet Nam's LCY government bond market remained the least diversified in the region. Insurance companies remained the largest investor group with a holdings share of 62.0% at the end of June, up from 61.5% a year earlier (**Figure 4**). This was followed by banks with a holdings share of 37.0%, slightly down from 37.5% during the same period. Collectively, these two dominant investor groups held 99.0% of LCY government bonds outstanding at the end of June, roughly unchanged from 99.1% a year earlier.

Sustainable Bond Market

The private sector remained the sole player in Viet Nam's sustainable bond market. At the end of June, private sector financing continued to dominate Viet Nam's sustainable bond market, which comprises green (52.2%) and sustainability bonds (47.8%) (**Figure 5**). Total outstanding sustainable bonds reached USD1.1 billion in Q2 2025. In terms of size, Viet Nam's sustainable bond market continued to lag behind its emerging East Asian peers, accounting for only 0.2% of the regional total. Outstanding sustainable bonds are predominantly short-term securities, mainly concentrated in tenors of 3 years and less (61.7%). The size-weighted average tenor stood at 2.4 years in Q2 2025, among the shortest tenors across the region's sustainable bond markets. Outstanding sustainable bonds were primarily denominated in United States dollars with a 54.8% share, followed by the Vietnamese dong with a 45.2% share.

www.ingramcontent.com/pod-product-compliance
Lightning Source LLC
Chambersburg PA
CBHW041800220926
51847CB00014B/274
* 9 7 8 9 2 9 2 7 7 4 3 6 3 *